Praise for *The Gospel of Simon*

"In a world where the media re   atred,
here is a quiet voice espousing the triumph of love and peace."
Archbishop Desmond Tutu, Nobel Peace Prize

"A book that reminds us again and again of Jesus's gospel of love."
Saul Bellow, Nobel Prize for Literature

"This book belongs among the classics of religion, if not in a class
all by itself. A masterpiece capable of changing the world."
W. P. Kinsella, author of *Field of Dreams*

"An ambitious reimagining of the most familiar story in history."
Chayym Zeldis, Tel Aviv University

"Smelcer gives us a Jesus who condemns those who abuse the
name of God to gain wealth or power, as well as anyone who
fosters injustice and inequality, oppresses others, and incites
hatred, intolerance, bigotry, and violence." Coretta Scott King

"John Smelcer challenges the certitudes of our times and offers a
blueprint for religious peace." Rabbi Joseph Ehrenkranz,
Center for Christian Jewish Understanding

"I've always wondered about Simon of Cyrene. It's nice to have this writer's imagination of his story." Barbara Cawthorne Crafton

"What moved me the most is Smelcer's emphasis, with much simplicity, on how our spirituality or faith can be a force for justice in the world." Victor Narro, UCLA Labor Center

"Like the original gospel writers, Smelcer uses the tale of Jesus to inspire. His challenge was to find a way into a story whose familiarity has made Christianity stale, judgmental, and dogmatic. He does so with brilliance and imagination, breathing new life into a faith that has forgotten simply to love." Rev. John C. Dorhauer, General Minister and President, United Church of Christ

"*The Gospel of Simon* presents a practical, approachable Jesus and brings the gospel narrative, and particularly the Sermon on the Mount, into a fresh perspective." Fr. Leo Walsh, S.T.D. Pontifical University of St. Thomas Aquinas, Rome

"My congratulations to John Smelcer for his imagination. I hope this book will help many people." Br. David Steindl-Rast

"In a world where the media relentlessly enflames fear and hatred, here is a quiet voice espousing the triumph of love and peace." —Archbishop Desmond Tutu, Nobel Peace Prize

"My friend, Thomas Merton, would have loved this elegantly simple, poetic, yet profound book that kindles the heart with what St. John of the Cross called The Flame of Love."
(formerly) Sister Mary Pius

"*The Gospel of Simon* presents the Jewish rabbi Jesus of Nazareth as the prophetic figure he undoubtedly was, at once embodying the wisdom of Judaism and emphasizing its message of lovingkindness and compassion. If only its universal message of peace and non-violence could prevail in every culture and reshape every political and economic system towards a world of generosity, caring for each other, and joyous celebration of our endangered planet."
Rabbi Michael Lerner, Editor of *Tikkun Magazine*

"Smelcer frees his imagination to create a moving narrative around one character who is almost a footnote in the Biblical story: Simon, who was compelled to carry Jesus' cross. In the process he reveals new dimensions in the Christian story." Bishop John Shelby Spong

"A daring retelling of 'The Greatest Story Ever Told' that is at once faithful yet radical in its reimagining." amazon.com

"A beautifully imagined life of Simon of Cyrene."
St. Anthony Messenger

"I've always wondered about Simon of Cyrene. It's nice to have this writer's imagination of his story." Barbara Cawthorne Crafton

"What moved me the most is Smelcer's emphasis, with much simplicity, on how our spirituality or faith can be a force for justice in the world." Victor Narro, UCLA Labor Center

"Like the original gospel writers, Smelcer uses the tale of Jesus to inspire. His challenge was to find a way into a story whose familiarity has made Christianity stale, judgmental, and dogmatic. He does so with brilliance and imagination, breathing new life into a faith that has forgotten simply to love." Rev. John C. Dorhauer, General Minister and President, United Church of Christ

"*The Gospel of Simon* presents a practical, approachable Jesus and brings the gospel narrative, and particularly the Sermon on the Mount, into a fresh perspective." Fr. Leo Walsh, S.T.D. Pontifical University of St. Thomas Aquinas, Rome

"My congratulations to John Smelcer for his imagination. I hope this book will help many people." Br. David Steindl-Rast

"In a world where the media relentlessly enflames fear and hatred, here is a quiet voice espousing the triumph of love and peace." —Archbishop Desmond Tutu, Nobel Peace Prize

The GOSPEL
of SIMON

John Smelcer

LEAP LF FAITH

The Gospel of Simon © 2016 by John Smelcer

Photograph © 2016 by Jim Caffrey

ISBN 978-0-692-79041-0

Global English Edition published by

LeapFaith Press in affiliation with

Leapfrog Press, P.O. Box 505

Fredonia, NY 14063 USA

www.thegospelofsimon.com

Library of Congress Cataloguing-in-Publications Data
Smelcer, John E., 1963-
The Gospel of Simon / John Smelcer. – Global English edition
The Passion and crucifixion of Jesus Christ as told by Simon of Cyrene.
ISBN 978-0-692-79041-0 (paperback, global edition)
[1. Fiction—Religious/Spiritual. 2. Fiction—Christian. 3. Fiction—Historical. 4. Christianity. 5. Jewish 6. Jesus. 7. Simon of Cyrene. 8. Holy Grail. 9. True Cross. 10. Biblical events—Fiction] I. Title.

Acknowledgements

This book is an inspired work of fiction, a creation of art, a fabrication from the imagination and intuition of one imperfect man. However, the storyline and historicity has been judiciously researched and contemplated by the author in collaboration with theologians in the hopes of creating something that is earnest, meaningful, affecting, and thought-provoking, something that deepens faith and belief and is not merely novelty. If it is anything, this is a book about love. Indeed, the word *love* or *loving* appears over a hundred times in this book.

While many people helped me along the way, I'd like to acknowledge the Stephen and Elaine McDuff, James O'Donnell, Dereck Daschke, Amber Johnson, John Jones, Helen Bar-Lev, Mary Shapiro, Charlotte LaGalle, Aaron Fine, José Carreno Medina, Chinua Achebe, Chayym Zeldis, Norman Mailer, Saul Bellow, Tom O'Horgan, Thich Nhat Hanh, the Dalai Lama, Marcus Borg, Tom Wright, Dan Berrigan, Cardinal Edward Egan, Billy Graham, Archbishop Desmond Tutu, Fr. Leo Walsh, Fr. William Kottenstette, Dale Stone, Barbara Cawthorne Crafton, Ronnaug and Danny Bull, Rod Clark, Helen Marie Grimes, Lisa Graziano, Joshua DeLeeuw, James Carroll, John Dorhauer, David Rambo, Bill Kinsella, Rabbi Michael Lerner, Rabbi Joseph

Ehrenkranz, Rabbi Rosenberg, Bishop John Shelby Spong, Bishop Edward Daly, Br. David Steindl-Rast, and my Harvard University professors: Ali Asani, Christopher Queen, and Helmut Koester. This is not to imply that they endorse the contents, opinions, or statements expressed herein.

This book is dedicated to Pope Francis for his gospel of love, mercy, charity, peace, inclusion, and environmental stewardship; to Martin Luther King Jr. for his peaceful struggle against racism and injustice, and to his friend Thomas Merton, who taught us to discard superficial gestures of religious zeal in favor of self-sacrificing love, "because our real journey in life is interior, of learning to surrender to the creative action of love and grace," for there can be no love of God that is divorced from charity, compassion, justice, or mercy.

Merton helped inform Martin Luther King Jr.'s practice of non-violent protest that was the hallmark of the Civil Rights Movement. Indeed, the two friends had planned a week-long spiritual retreat at Merton's hermitage in Kentucky, but King was assassinated a month before the scheduled event. Merton himself died under mysterious circumstance in Thailand eight months later. All three exemplify the Christian obligation to seek peace, relieve suffering, and correct injustice. In his address to the U. S. Congress on September 24, 2015, Pope Francis praised Thomas Merton and Martin Luther King Jr. as being among the greatest Americans, alongside Dorothy Day and Abraham Lincoln.

Prologue

Inasmuch as any writing is said to be inspired, the idea for this book began one wintry night in Alaska in 1996. I was standing outside my little cabin at thirty degrees below zero, gazing awestruck at the northern lights dancing across a sky full of stars, the flickering yellow light from an oil lamp on a table beside the window casting a square on the snow. It was at that moment the vision came to me. But I wasn't yet a novelist. I didn't know *how* to tell such a story. I might even have been fearful of the vision.

Who was I to write such a book?

So, I carried the insistent story inside me like a like an agonizing secret. For years, some friends discouraged me from writing this book, while others like Saul Bellow, Chayym Zeldis, and Norman Mailer encouraged me to write it. Mailer, who helped me develop the overall structure of the novel, joked that if I didn't write it, he would. More than once, I discussed the project with Tom O'Horgan in his Manhattan loft. Tom had directed Andrew Lloyd Webber's Broadway rock operas, *Jesus Christ Superstar* and *Hair*.

Over the years, the novel had many false starts as I wrestled with how to tell Simon's story and how we came to hold it in our hands. I wrote a dozen different beginnings. I sought advice from conservative and liberal Catholic and Protestant clergy and from the world's greatest biblical scholars, as well as from leaders of other religions so that I might create a book of universal appeal.

I wrote to Nobel Peace Prize winners Archbishop Desmond Tutu and the Dalai Lama. After all, the book's message of love, selflessness, compassion, peace, and tolerance are central tenets of Buddhism (and besides, the Dalai Lama has always been very respectful of the life and message of Jesus). Similarly, I wrote to the Vietnamese Zen Buddhist teacher, Thich Nhat Hanh, who, along with Thomas Merton, helped to inform Martin Luther King Jr.'s notions of peaceful resistance during the Civil Rights Movement. In 1967, King nominated Hanh for the Nobel Peace Prize for his efforts to end the war in Vietnam.

I shared drafts of the manuscript with Billy Graham, Chinua Achebe, Coretta Scott King, Bishop John Shelby Spong, Rabbi Michael Lerner, Rabbi Joseph Ehrenkranz, Barbara Cawthorne Crafton, Archbishop Joseph Kurtz, Bishop Edward Daly, Daniel Berrigan, Cardinal Edward Egan, N. T. Wright, and Marcus Borg. I had the honor of meeting Archbishop Kurtz in Louisville. I met Cardinal Egan, Dan Berrigan, and Rabbi Ehrenkranz in New York City. I met Bishop Daly in Dublin and Bishop Wright in Durham, England, and I met Marcus Borg in the fall of 2005 when he and John Dominic Crossan and their families visited Alaska. It was

Marcus who suggested that I only use the Gospel of Mark to frame the historicity of the novel.

I wrote to Jewish friends in Israel and to rabbinical scholars around the world asking for their help so that I might not perpetuate stereotypes. After all, Jesus was first and foremost a Jew, and the story of the Passion is largely a Jewish narrative. I asked folks not to discuss what I was writing with anyone else. Keeping my cards close to the vest, I never told anyone about the ending of the book, though I had envisioned it since the beginning.

It was my secret.

Despite my insecurities and trepidations, I felt compelled to write this book. I believed in it. To that end, I researched the topic assiduously. Over several years, I enrolled in graduate courses in religion at Harvard University, including a class on the historical Jesus. My professor was the distinguished biblical scholar, Helmut Koester.

Yet, overcome at times with doubt, still I did not finish the book. I prayed that one day I would. I also prayed that I would write it without agenda, promising myself that I would abandon the project if I felt a single word was disingenuous. Sometimes, while writing the book, I felt a kind of exhilaration bordering on manic, as if I couldn't write fast enough to produce it, the writing better than my abilities. Nightly, I awoke from dreams, excitedly scribbling down what I could remember. Of all my books to date, writing *The Gospel of Simon* has certainly been the most intense and rewarding experience. Omnis via est ad finem.

The GOSPEL
of SIMON

"The soldiers compelled a passerby, who was coming in from the country, to carry his cross; it was Simon of Cyrene, father of Alexander and Rufus." (Mark 15: 20-22)

IT HAD BEEN A HATEFUL DAY, full of spite and tension. From the arguments in the office and the lunatic on the street corner shouting how everyone was wicked and condemned to hell, to the news of yet another suicide bombing and massacre on the radio during the sweltering bumper-to-bumper ride home, where the jerk in the car behind him was blasting his horn the whole time, it seemed like a day when all kindness and tolerance in the world was put on hold.

Simon just wanted to be done with it. He wanted to go home, change out of his suit, and have something cold to drink before his date that evening. But just before he got there, his grandfather called, begging him to drop by.

"Please," he had said. "I need to talk to you about something."

Simon's frustration showed when he finally walked through the door with his tie loosened around his neck and as he paced his grandfather's small living room, while the old man went to fetch something from the bedroom.

Finally, his grandfather came out with a wooden box, only a little larger than a shoe box, which he gently placed on the small kitchen table. He pulled out a chair and gestured for him to sit down.

"I can't stay long, Grandpa. I just dropped by for a few minutes because you asked me to. I need to go home and change. I'm meeting Rebekah at Café Hillel in an hour and then we're going to the free concert at Jerusalem Theatre this evening."

"Your generation is always busy, always in a hurry. It's bad for your health. You need to learn to slow down. You should pray for patience."

"You know I don't go to church anymore, Grandpa. It always seemed so insincere and . . . pointless," Simon said, thinking of the right word. "And I don't pray, either. I see all the suffering and injustice and violence in the world, the genocide and mass shootings that are so commonplace we have become indifferent to them, and the never-ending wars, which almost always have religious hatred at the root. Why doesn't God stop it?"

"It's not that simple," began the old man. "God gave us . . ."

But the grandson interrupted before he could finish.

"I'm sick and tired of the hypocrisy of people who use religion to oppress the rights of others and to inflict suffering, and of people screaming how we're all condemned to hell if we believe differently. Religion's all about hate. I don't believe in any of it anymore."

"But not everyone's like that."

"Yes they are! Every time I turn on the television there's news of a brutal massacre in the name of religion or of some scandal or corruption. On the radio some bigoted political or religious fanatic is spouting fear and hatred. Violence and greed has become our religion. Nowadays, it's every man for himself. Just take what you can and the hell with everyone else," he said, thinking of the two-faced co-worker who was gunning for his job.

"What you say is true," replied the old man. "There is a lot of that. But people have become lost. More than ever we need to . . ."

"Look!" interrupted the grandson again. "There is no God. There was no Jesus. No cross. There is no love . . . only hate. I got to go."

The old man's expression turned to sorrow for his grandson. He sighed before speaking.

"Sit down. Please. I've been waiting a long time to show you something."

The younger man studied his grandfather's face, saw the earnestness. He took a deep breath and bit his lower lip.

"All right," he said reluctantly, reaching into his pocket for his cell phone. "I'll tell Rebekah that I have to cancel our date. But it better be important."

"It is," replied the old man with a sudden hopeful smile.

While his grandson sent a text message to his girlfriend, the old man turned off the television and opened the window by the little kitchen table, the blue curtains billowing in the summer breeze. Through the window, he could see the little stone goat house at the edge of his fenced yard. He used to own more land, but he'd sold most of it to a developer fifteen years ago, keeping only a small lot that included the house and the goat house, which had been on the land for so many generations no one knew how old it was for certain.

What used to be his family's farm was now surrounded by houses, each similar to the next and all of them painted white, clean and bright in the sunshine. Beyond the old goat house, he could see the beige drabness of sand and rock and the ancient rolling hills sparsely clad in scrubby, green trees with overcrowded housing and ugly power lines running toward Jerusalem in the distance.

"All right, Grandpa. Rebekah said she'll take a raincheck. She said there's a movie she wanted to see anyhow. So what is it you want to show me?"

The old man patted one of the two wooden chairs at the small table.

"Come sit," he said happily.

When they were both seated, the young man across from his grandfather, the old man pulled the box closer.

"This is older than you can imagine," he said, removing the lid and carefully setting it aside.

A musty smell arose from the opened box.

"What is it?"

"Your past. Your future."

Simon looked puzzled.

The old man lifted out a bundle of paper tied crisscross with blue twine.

Simon stood up and leaned over to get a better glimpse. From where he stood, he could see what looked like a leather bound book still inside the box.

His grandfather laid a wrinkled hand atop the pages.

"This manuscript contains the story of our family, our place in history."

The grandson struggled to understand what his grandfather was talking about. As far as he knew there was nothing special about their family, no claim to fame, let alone some extraordinary role in history.

"I'm getting old. I must tell you a secret while my mind is still clear."

Simon wondered if the bundle of papers was his grandfather's journal.

"Is it about when you were young, about something you did? The war, maybe?" he asked, sitting back down.

"No."

"Is it about my dad? Was he adopted?"

The old man chuckled, the wrinkles around his eyes like deep canyons etched by floodwater.

"No."

"Is it about Grandma, how you met her?"

The old man smiled softly. He missed his wife.

"No. It's not about your grandmother. No more questions. The secret I must share with you happened long before I was born. It's the story of what happened to the first Simon, for whom we are both named."

The old man pushed the manuscript across the table to his grandson.

"Read this. There's time enough."

Simon thumbed randomly through a few pages. The manuscript looked as if it were typed on onion-skin paper on one of those old, manual typewriters.

"I'll be in the goat house when you're done."

Simon untied the twine and set aside the blank first page. As he began to read, his grandfather shuffled across the creaking floor to the door, grabbing his cane and a worn, black fedora from a hook on the wall beside a small wooden crucifix. He glanced back just as Simon looked up from the manuscript as if startled, his mouth agape, his eyes questioning.

The old man tipped his hat at his grandson and smiled before stepping into the sunlight.

MY NAME IS SIMON. I WAS BORN IN CYRENE, a seaside city in the province of Cyrenaica not far from the Roman seaport of Apollonia on the southern Mediterranean coast. My family moved to Judaea when I was a boy. My mother died at sea on the journey. My father bought some land less than a half a day's journey from Jerusalem on which he could raise goats and grow olives and a vineyard.

But this story is not about that.

It is about the day I helped a Nazarene named Jesus carry his cross through the streets of Jerusalem up to Golgotha where he was crucified.

It has been forty years since that day, more or less. I was much stronger and taller than I am now. I asked my grandson to write down my recollections for me while I still remember clearly. Ezra learned to write in Aramaic. I promised him one of my goats for his labor, a pregnant nanny.

What you are about to read I have told few others.

You will doubt some of what I say. You may even think I am lying. That is understandable. You were not there. It is difficult for most people to believe things they have not seen with their own eyes.

For my own part, I forgive you your skepticism.

Thursday

"Love is the fulfillment of the law."

Romans 13:10

MY FATHER DIED WHEN HE WAS FORTY-SEVEN, and I inherited this land, which I have lived on ever since. Back when this story began, I lived here with my wife, Rachel, and my two sons—Alexander and Rufus. On this particular Passover, my firstborn, Alexander, was seventeen. Rufus was fifteen. Like their father, they were sturdy boys who would become strong men. Our daughter, Avigail, was four at the time.

Avigail was deathly sick. Sometimes, her fever burned like a fire. When the fever was very high, her little body convulsed in violent fits, her eyes rolling back in her head, which always terrified her mother. Avigail's stomach wouldn't hold down food or drink. Her mother was always cleaning up after her, washing rags. Our little daughter was wasting away, and nothing we did seemed to help. The village healer had been consulted, but none of her remedies cured the sickness. I felt as helpless as a feather on the Jordan, hopeless in the certainty our beautiful, little daughter was going to die.

I was kneeling beside Avigail's bed, wiping her burning body with a wet cloth, when Alexander and Rufus returned from the field, where they had been laboring since morning.

"How is our sister?" asked Alexander.

"She is getting worse," I said sadly, shaking my head. "She hasn't opened her eyes all day."

Rufus knelt beside Avigail and placed a hand on her forehead.

"Get well, Little One," he whispered. "May God take pity on you."

Avigail's eyes did not move.

"Did you boys repair the wheel on the cart, like I asked? Tomorrow is Passover. We must take the wine into Jerusalem to sell."

The boys said the cart was repaired.

"Very good," I replied. "And how goes it with the goat house?"

"We have laid down the first four courses of stone," replied Alexander. "The stones are well fit. It's a strong foundation."

Rufus nodded in agreement with his older brother.

I kissed Avigail on the forehead.

"Come," I said, rising from my knees, "let's go see your handiwork and load the cart for tomorrow's journey."

Outside, I stopped on a small rise and looked down over my land, marveling at the grove of olive trees and the neat rows of grape vines laid down by my father. My sons stood beside me, one on either side. From where we stood, we could see the vertical stone wheel that pressed oil from our olives and the little garden where my wife grew vegetables and herbs for our family. Goats grazed in the vineyard and chickens scratched in the soil. We could also see the beginning of the new goat house beside the old, collapsed wooden one. Built of stones, the new goat house would last for many generations.

"This is good land," I said. "I can be proud to pass it to you one day. Hopefully, you will pass it on to your sons."

I followed my boys to the cart to inspect the wheel, looking closely at the repair. I grabbed the rim and pulled on it to check how well it was connected to the axle. The wheel was tight, the hub well-greased.

"A fine job," I said, patting both of my sons on the shoulder. "Now, help me load the wine into the cart."

I had twenty amphorae, each as high as a tall man's waist filled with wine and sealed with wax to prevent spilling or spoilage. My sons helped me to lift each clay vessel into the cart. The tall amphorae stood like soldiers against each other in such a manner that they did not fall over. They were used in trade ships because they could be stacked in the hold, with the added purpose of serving as ballast on rough seas.

Rufus almost dropped one as he hoisted it up to me, but he caught it in time.

"Careful," I admonished him. "Each of these is very valuable, especially during Passover when there is great demand for wine."

When the amphorae were loaded, we shoved straw between the spaces to prevent breakage from jostling in the cart on the road to Jerusalem.

"Now, let us go see the goat house," I said, wiping sweat from my brow with the back of my hand.

The first four courses were set, rising almost waist high. I examined the opening I had marked for the door.

"I couldn't have done better myself," I said. "After one more course of stones, make a window here." I placed a small rock on the stone wall to mark the place.

Just then, Rachel called to us from the house.

Jacob and Aliza, an elderly couple who had a small farm in the next valley, had come to visit. Their sons and daughters had long since married and moved away to begin their own families. Their granddaughter, Nessa, was about Alexander's age. They had come to see how Avigail's health was. Aliza brought a poultice she said would cure our daughter's sickness. She said it must first be submerged in warm water. After Aliza had squeezed out the water, my wife led Aliza to our daughter's bedside, where she pulled back the bedding and placed the damp bag of aromatic herbs on Avigail's chest, close to her neck.

"She will breathe in the healing vapors," Aliza said. "I used this on my own children when they were sick. It will help, you will see."

While our little girl lay in her bed breathing in the medicine, we sat at the table and talked for a while.

"Tell me, Simon, are you still going into Jerusalem tomorrow?" asked Jacob.

"Yes. The wine is already loaded for the journey."

"May you profit," said Jacob. "Are your sons going with you?"

"Yes."

"Then," said Jacob to Rachel, "you must call on us if you need any help while they are away."

"Much thanks to you," she replied. "May God smile on both of you."

Before leaving, Jacob took me aside where my wife could not hear.

"Perhaps your daughter's ailment is retribution for violating one of God's laws," he said. "Can you think of anything? Perhaps you have eaten something that was not kosher or your wife has despoiled the sacrament of the mikvah?"

"I have wondered so myself," I replied, thinking of Job's false comforters. "But why punish Avigail?"

That night, after throwing away the ineffective poultice, my wife and I lay in bed talking about the next day, quietly so as not to wake our sons who slept nearby.

"Perhaps, if I fetch a good price for the wine, I can pay a more skilled healer from Jerusalem to come help Avigail."

I knew that I could only pay so much because most of the money would have to support my family until the fall when the olives would be pressed for their oil.

Rachel squeezed my hand gently in the darkness.

"That would be wonderful," she whispered. "Perhaps the pain in your head could be cured as well."

For many years, I had suffered frequent pain in my head. The aching—especially when it was behind my eyes—was such that I felt I would retch and wish that I would die. It was so unbearable that all I could do was to lay in bed in the dark with my eyes closed, unable to work. At such times, my loving wife would sit beside me and rub my temples and knead the back of my neck, which always seemed to help a little. Avigail, before she became sick, would sometimes rub my temples and neck as she had seen her mother do and say, "Does that feel better, Father?"

"Then let us pray that I get a good price. It is a half day's journey each way. We will leave before sunrise. Time to sleep."

I kissed my wife and rolled over.

Friday

"In this shall everyone know that you are my disciples:
if you have love for one another."

John 13:35

WE LEFT BENEATH A SKY FULL OF STARS. As I walked out the door, careful to close it gently, I touched the mezuzah mounted on the doorway. In darkness, my sons and I harnessed our donkey to the cart loaded with wine. As we began our uneventful journey to the city, aided by the light of a full moon, my thoughts were of Avigail and how I might earn enough extra money from the wine to hire someone to help her.

She was so sweet before her affliction. Her smile was like a bright lamp in the darkness. Her laughter when I tickled her was the most joyous sound in the world. She loved for me to carry her on my shoulders, and some mornings I would awake to find her nuzzled in bed between me and my wife. I would give my life for hers, if such a sacrifice could be made for another.

My plan was to get in and out of the city as quickly as possible.

As I led the way, my sons walked behind me half asleep.

Our spirits arose with the sun that cast a golden light upon the green hills and valleys, alive with springtime grass and flowers.

We arrived early in the morning. The merchants in the marketplace were setting up their stalls for the busy day.

I hate going into Jerusalem.

It is always crowded and noisy, especially during the Holy Week of Passover when thousands of Jews flock to the bustling city to worship and to make sacrifice at the Temple, their tents cluttering the grounds outside the city walls. The smell of waste from so many people and the smoke from so many burnt offerings is disagreeable to my nose. Give me the fresh air and serenity of my farm.

I only go into the city when I need to sell wine or olive oil or to buy things.

Among the multitude are the prophets who usually wander the countryside. It seems that everyone is a prophet nowadays. The country is full of them, preaching *this* or *that*, shouting and spitting their messages of impending doom, most of them half mad. Then there are the zealots plotting rebellion to overthrow the Romans. If that isn't enough, there are the countless exorcists and magicians who masquerade as miracle workers—most of them charlatans who earn their living from the despair and suffering of others. And then there are the wretched beggars and pickpockets, many of them children, who ply their slippery craft on unwary pilgrims.

If you ask me, the high priests at the Temple are the worst of them, filling their purses and treasury and impoverishing others by ransoming access to God. Every day, the sick who are too poor to pay their exorbitant fees perish from their illnesses. During Passover, the priests double the fee to make a sacrifice, which they require of every Jew. It is extortion. What does God need of gold and silver? He could make a mountain of it. In the name of God, the priests steal the homes of widows to support the lavish palace of the high priest.

Greed and power have made the high priests like prancing peacocks who preen and lavish themselves with offerings earned from the labors and sufferings of other Jews. They are more concerned with how people address them in the market and where they sit at feasts than with the welfare of others. They debase their office. They have forgotten that being Jewish is both privilege and a responsibility. They have become tools of the Roman Empire. The high priests taint the Temple and violate the laws of God as given to Moses.

Thou shalt not steal.

Thou shalt not covet.

And most important:

Love your neighbor as yourself.

Their avarice is without bounds, made all the worse by their troubling association with the Romans, who uphold the precarious peace in Jerusalem by crucifying runaway slaves and rebel dissidents and leaving their rotting corpses as warning to others and for the ever-present crows and vultures and scavenging dogs who feed on them until there is nothing left to bury.

Judaea is wretched with the ghastly spectacle.

You could throw out the whole lot of them for all I care. I give them a wide berth for most of the year. I come here only to sell my goods. I always return to my farm in haste after the wine or olive oil is sold for a good price.

I sold half the wine quickly. Though I haggled for more, I got less than I had hoped for. I was told again and again there was a glut of wine this year and prices were down with so much wine to be had. With my purse lighter than I had expected, I worried that I might not be able to find a healer to help Avigail.

When we were close to the Temple, I left my sons to guard our possessions while I went inside to make an offering to God, as required during Passover, but especially on behalf of my daughter. In spite of my feelings about the high priests, I still sought to obey

God's laws. While I was waiting in line to purchase an animal to sacrifice, the man in front of me turned and spoke to me.

"Look at all the pilgrims come here to sacrifice," he said.

I turned and looked back at the throng of people.

"There are a great many," I replied.

"God demands a sea of blood," he said, smiling, though most of his teeth were missing or rotten. "His blood thirst is insatiable."

Of course, the priests wanted to lighten my purse for the privilege of sacrifice. I tried to plead with one of them, telling him that the loss of so many coins could mean the difference between life and death for my Avigail.

He did not care.

"You must pay the tribute price or no sacrifice."

I tried to appeal to his compassion.

"But it is just a dove, not a lamb. The last time I came here it cost half as much to sacrifice a dove. Surely you can help a worried father," I said.

"If I do it for you, others will expect the same, and then where would we be?"

"Please," I pleaded. "I must save some money for my daughter."

"You offend God with your excuses," he said coldly, turning to the next person in line.

"*You* offend God!" I replied angrily, as I turned and left the Temple.

Once outside in the sunlight, I found Alexander and Rufus where I had instructed them to wait for me.

"Come, my sons," I said, grabbing the rope around the donkey's neck. "Let us sell the last of the wine and find a healer for your sister so we can leave this accursed city."

We pushed on through the crowd to a lane busy with commotion.

With so many people lining the narrow lane on both sides, it was impossible to cross to the other side.

"What is happening?" I asked someone.

"The Romans are crucifying a man from Nazareth. He comes this way even now," he said pointing.

I pressed a little closer so that I was able to see a man trudging my way, struggling to carry a heavy cross. His face was bloodied from a crown of thorns, his long hair a mop of blood. The burden of the heavy cross was too much for him. As I watched, he crumpled beneath it. Three centurions stood over him shouting at him.

"Get up!" the tallest soldier barked in broken Aramaic as he whipped the hapless man.

"Get up, dog!" screamed the one with a scar across his cheek and eye.

The shortest soldier kicked the man.

Onlookers on both sides of the lane jeered, their faces twisted in a frenzy of hatred. I saw one man throw a glancing stone at him.

The bloodied man tried to rise, but he collapsed again, the weight of the cross smashing his face against the cobblestones.

He did not move.

I thought he was dead.

It was then that I saw his back. I have seen my share of the horrors the Romans are capable of inflicting on the body, but I have never seen anything like the scourging of this man's back. It was as if a lion had ripped away every piece of flesh until his ribs were exposed.

One of the centurions rolled him over to see if he was still alive.

It was then that I saw that his chest had been lashed almost as savagely as his back. His arms and legs were crisscrossed with bleeding stripes. I wondered if there was no place on this man's body that was not lashed by scourge or whip.

As I watched, the man struggled to his knees.

I was amazed that he was still alive, so much did he resemble a corpse.

Just then the shorter centurion approached me.

"You there! Come here!" he demanded, sizing me up.

I looked around, thinking he meant someone else. But then he grabbed me brusquely and pulled me from the crowd.

"You look strong as an ox. Get over there and help the dog carry his cross."

I protested, but the soldier pulled his short sword and thrust it against my chest.

"It will be *my* neck if he dies before he is crucified."

"What is that to me?" I replied.

"You dare defy a Roman?" he growled.

I sized up the man. Though he had a sword, he was no match for me. I was a head taller and many stones heavier. I could break his neck as a dry twig. But that would only bring the wrath of the Roman Empire upon my family. How would it help Avigail if I were imprisoned?

Alexander grabbed my arm from behind.

"What is it, Father? What is happening?" he asked.

"Stay here with the cart," I said, as I pulled the money purse from beneath my garment and gave it to him. "Guard this and the wine."

As the centurion pulled me away I could hear Alexander yelling for me.

"Father! Father!"

"I will be back!" I turned and shouted. "Do as I say!"

I straddled the fallen man and raised the cross from him. It was heavy, even for a strong man such as I was back then. With the long beam braced against a shoulder, I reached a helping hand to the man.

"Get up," I said. "Your burden is lifted."

"Not yet," I heard him whisper, as he struggled to his feet and steadied himself against me.

The short centurion snapped his whip at us. The lashing end bit into my calf.

"Get moving!" he demanded, drawing his arm back as if to whip me again.

I turned and glowered at the man, who held his hand.

With the cross astride my left shoulder and my left hand gripping it, I held my right arm around the weak man's waist to support him. Together, with our arms around the other, we stumbled along the way, the rough-hewn beam rasping the flesh from my shoulder. It was then that I noticed the wound on the shoulder of my companion. The abrasive beam had stripped away all flesh and laid bare the bone.

I shuddered at the thought of the unbearable agony he must be suffering.

As we staggered past the raucous spectators, the man occasionally looked up at my face, as if to see what manner of man I was.

At such times, I had to look away, unable to endure the depth of sorrow I saw.

But there was something more than sorrow there. For nearly forty years, I have tried to comprehend what I saw in his eyes that day. I cannot describe it. It was not despair or profound dread, as you might imagine. I think what I saw, what I *felt* in his glance, was *Love*. But how does one *see* love? We witness it in deeds; we hear it spoken in words. But I swear I *saw* love residing within his sorrow.

I stand by it, though you think I am an old fool.

Our going was slow. I worried about my sons, but I knew that they would obey me.

At one point I spoke to my companion.

"What is your crime to be punished so brutally?" I asked. "It must be heinous. Are you a murderer?"

"I am a teacher."

Even his teeth were bloodied.

I looked over the man again, at his terrible wounds, skeptical that a teacher would be so tortured.

"Surely Pilate is not crucifying rabbis for teaching," I asked, concerned that the Romans might be imposing new laws on Judaea that restricted our religion.

"My crime is treason," said the man.

For some distance, I wondered what he could have taught that was treasonous. Finally, when we were stopped while the centurions ordered some spectators to push a broken cart out of the way, I asked him.

"What did you teach?"

"My father's message."

I remember wondering what it was his father must have said that the son was so punished. I had never heard of a son being punished for his father's crime.

Bystanders and passersby continuously jeered and mocked the man, shaking angry fists. This far from Herod's Palace, I wondered if they even knew this man's crime. Surely they could not all have heard Pilate's sentence. Besides, with so many pilgrims in the city for Passover, I suspected that a good many of the spectators weren't even from Jerusalem. All they saw was a man carrying the all too familiar instrument of his destruction.

And so they taunted and tormented him.

One man spat on him. When I scowled at him, he cowered back into the hissing throng.

Another man flung a handful of donkey dung, which struck me as well. I dropped the heavy cross and grabbed the man by his neck until his eyes bulbed in his head.

"I am not a criminal like him," I snarled, shaking the man like a rag and straw doll.

Just then the centurions grabbed me and made me release the man, who fell to his knees choking and holding his hands to his throat. At sword point they forced me back to the cross.

"Pick it up! Move on!" ordered the soldier with the scar on his face.

As I bent over the cross, the rabbi said to me, "Do not hate them, but love them and forgive them as I do."

I looked at him curiously as I heaved the bloodied cross to my shoulder. By now, the roughness of the beam was laying bare the flesh of my shoulder. Already my tunic was covered with his blood, and now his blood mingled with my own.

"Where are your followers, Rabbi?" I asked, cringing as the cross slid down my shoulder like a rasp. "Are there no friendly faces amidst the crowd?"

The rabbi's countenance became sadder, if that were possible.

"They who love me, have abandoned me. I fear it will always be so. But I forgive them, for fear is a tyrant."

I looked at him, this broken shell of a man, with a mounting pity. He was marching with only a stranger to his certain and long and painful death. How lonely he must feel; a dead man walking among the living.

"I'm sorry," is all I managed to reply.

I felt his arm tighten around my waist, as if in embrace.

"Love is God's greatest gift," he said, "but it is also the most tenuous."

Just then a woman bolted toward us from the line of onlookers. With a cloth she wiped blood and sweat from the rabbi's face as she wept. Almost immediately, the scar-faced centurion pulled her away and shoved her roughly to the cobblestones. She clutched the bloodied cloth even as she fell.

"Keep back, woman!" he yelled. "All of you . . . keep back!" he shouted at the mob, brandishing his sword.

I watched as the woman arose to her feet, kissed the cloth, and vanished into the scowling multitude.

"It seems you have one friend still," I said.

The rabbi nodded weakly.

"Blessed are women," he replied feebly, "for they are the Mercy Givers."

I was beginning to respect this man. Even now, his heart did not harbor hate or resentment. Nor was there fear in his eyes.

Nothing he said or did seemed seditious to me. Nothing he said seemed to threaten Rome's peace. I began to question his guilt.

Perhaps the Romans had made a mistake.

Almost as if he had heard my thoughts, my companion looked up at me kindly.

Just then he stumbled.

With my strong right hand clasping his, I raised up the man yet again, and held him closer to me so that I might better support his frailty. By now not only was my tunic soaked with his blood, the hair on my right arm was matted with it.

As he stood, I saw him press his cheek against the rough wood and kiss it. I'm certain he was unaware that I had seen. Where his lips touched, I noted a knot in the wood and a tool mark made by the woodworker's draw-knife as he hewed the beam.

Together, we pushed on again. At times the crowd pressed upon us so that we could scarcely move. At such times, the centurions dispersed them.

The soldiers whipped the rabbi when he did not move fast enough.

Sometimes they whipped him anyway.

Several times their wicked lashings found the flesh of my back, instead of his. I could feel the warm blood beneath my tunic.

And through it all, despite his mortal injuries, the man continued with a strength of will as constant as the stars. I couldn't understand what kept the man going. He was already dead. Why did he not just quit and die on the path instead of suffering the agonizing crucifixion that awaited?

"How is it you keep going?" I asked.

I did not understand his answer.

"His will be done, not mine."

I imagined he meant Pilate.

As we approached the city gate, I spied a man kneeling along the way surrounded by the scornful bystanders. His face was wet with tears and his countenance abounding with sorrow.

The rabbi saw him, too.

As we passed, their eyes locked in embrace, and the man on his knees burst into lamentation as if *he* were the one hoisting the cross, as if it were *his* flesh that was torn from his body. I shall never be able to forget the grief engraved on his face and a sorrow as lonely and desolate as a castaway afloat in the middle of a raging sea.

One of the centurion's whips found my back.

"Keep moving!"

After passing, I asked about the man.

"Was that one of your followers?"

"He is my brother, James."

I thought about the sorrowfulness of brother witnessing the insufferable torment of brother. Such grief must be unbearable.

"I thought your followers had all forsaken you?"

"All but James. My brother alone has not abandoned me, and yet shall my followers abandon him."

Again, I did not fathom his meaning.

I looked back in time to see the brother of this man, the one he called James, stand and wipe his face with a hand, and then vanish into the raucous crowd.

There were fewer spectators once we passed through the gate and beyond the wall of the city, mostly pilgrims who were camped outside. Ahead of us, the winding way led through a vineyard and up a rocky hillside with hollows in its craggy face that made it resemble a skull.

They call the place Golgotha, a fitting name.

The stony path ahead grew steep. The soldiers ordered us to stop at the base so that we could muster our strength for the final push upward. I think the break was for their benefit, not ours. One of them had gone back to fetch a pail of water.

I stood straight, stretching my aching back. The Rabbi rested on his knees with one hand holding on to my tunic for support.

"Almost there," I said, gazing at the lofty crest bounded by a blue sky.

He did not answer.

I turned to look.

With his eyes closed, the man was swaying gently, his head moving as one rapt in prayer.

"Rabbi?"

He did not answer.

I shook him, careful to touch the shoulder that was not savaged.

Slowly, as if awakening from a dream, he opened his eyes and looked up at me.

"Do you not hear that?" he said.

I heard nothing but the wind in the trees and the soldiers complaining.

"What?"

"That music."

I strained to listen.

"I hear nothing."

"It sounds like the music of Heaven. That is why birds sing. They remember the beautiful music of the Creator, the sound of

Heaven. That is how it is with prayer: all prayers ascend to God as song; the multitude of prayers arising in a chorus."

I have heard how some people are said to see or hear things at the moment of their death.

Just then one of the centurions shouted at us to get a move on.

"The hill is not getting any smaller!"

I hoisted the cursed cross upon my raw shoulder, repositioning it to get a better grip on it.

"Come," I said, pulling my companion to his feet. "It is almost done."

With his scourged and whip-torn arm around my shoulder, we began our ascent with renewed vigor. I swear it was as if *he* were pulling me onward. I marveled at his strength, at his commitment despite the horrors that awaited him at the hilltop. His was no coward's soul.

There were more centurions awaiting us at the top. There were also two naked men already crucified.

The soldiers took the burden of the cross from me and pushed me to the ground.

Instantly, they seized the rabbi, stripped him naked, and dragged him upon the cross. From practice, centurions at each point of the cross pulled his arms and feet into position.

From my knees, my hands clutching fistfuls of earth, I watched intently as one of the soldiers took up an iron mallet and a long iron spike.

"Stretch it further!" he barked at the soldier holding the rabbi's right hand. "Hold it still!"

He was just about to drive the spike when he noticed me.

"You!" he shouted, brandishing the mallet. "Go home! Unless you want some of this."

One of the other centurions took up his lance and threatened me.

I scrambled to my feet and backed away.

From where I stood, I could see my companion's bloody face. His mouth moved, but no word ushered from his lips. Still, I knew that he had said to me, "Go."

I do not know how to describe the feelings that welled inside me. After our dreadful journey together—me mostly wishing that I had never been forced to help this man—I found myself feeling something like . . . kinship. Although I wanted to stay with him to the end, I had no desire to witness the horrible suffering he was about to endure. His body had already suffered enough. But then I thought of my two sons waiting for me and of my little daughter back home whose life depended on me. I could not leave them to grow up without a father.

As I struggled with my desire both to flee and to stay, I saw the rabbi nod, telling me without words that it was all right for me to leave.

I turned and ran down the steep path, the sound of the clanking mallet ringing in my ears pushing me ever faster down the hill. In my haste, I almost crashed into two women coming up the path, the oldest accompanied by a young man who steadied her.

"Forgive me," I said as we passed.

I ran all the way back to the city without looking back, my fear and guilt pushing me headlong like a hard wind.

I found my sons where I had left them. No misfortune had befallen them. They were alarmed when they saw my tunic soaked in blood, the reddish brown blood dried on my arms and hands, the streaks of blood on my tunic from the lashings on my back, and the blood-soaked place on my shoulder.

I told them that it was not my blood and not to worry.

After more assurances that I was unharmed, Alexander related how he had sold five amphorae of wine, haggling a slightly better price for them than I had for the others. I looked at the cart and saw that there were only five vessels remaining. Alexander handed back the coin purse.

"You will make a shrewd merchant," I said.

"Come," I said, taking the reins of the donkey. "Let us sell the rest of the wine and find a healer for your sister so we can go home."

It took almost two hours to sell the wine. By then it was noonday. We ate a midday meal, and I purchased an iron cooking pot for my wife. She had asked me to fetch one home. With a purse full of coins we went in search of a healer. But none would accompany us home for the price I could afford to pay.

They all told me the same thing.

"Your house is too far away. It would take a day to go there and back. If I go with you, I will earn only the little sum you offer. With all the pilgrims in the city this week looking for healers, I can make ten times that amount if I stay. Besides, the Sabbath begins at sundown. It is forbidden to work or travel."

I knew that we had to get home before sunset. As I have said, I was a good Jew, observant of the laws.

No matter how urgently I pleaded my daughter's condition or explained that I had to keep enough money for my family to live on until the olives were pressed in the fall, no healer would accompany us. Increasingly distraught, I offered the last healer more money than I could afford and suggested that he come after the Sabbath.

He too waved me aside and laughed.

With a heavy heart, certain that my daughter would die, I returned home with my sons. As I walked behind them in silence, exhausted from my ordeal and feeling every wound on my stiffening body, especially the lashes on my back, I thought about the unexpected events of the day. I also thought about where we would bury Avigail. There was a pretty spot in the olive grove beside a large stone. She always liked the place. Often she asked to eat our midday meal there.

Then I wondered about the man I had left on the cross.

Who was he?

We made it home before sundown. Rachel ran out from the house distraught with worry when she saw me.

"What happened? Were you robbed?"

"Be still, wife," I said, trying to reassure her, though I must have appeared a fright. "The blood is not mine. How is our daughter?"

"She is awake. She has been asking for you."

I went straight to Avigail's bedside. She smiled weakly when she saw me leaning over her.

"Your father is home," I said with a smile and softly squeezed her hand.

She took my blood-caked hand and caressed it against her feverish cheek. But although she seemed slightly better, her eyes seemed dimmer than ever. I worried she would not last through the night.

A hot tear ran down my cheek.

"Everything is going to be all right," I lied.

She kissed my hand.

While Alexander and Rufus put away the cart and fed and watered the donkey, Rachel carefully undressed me. She grimaced on seeing the welts on my back and the horrible wound to my shoulder.

"How did this happen? Who did this to you?" she asked.

"I will tell you tonight after the boys are asleep."

"I do not think this is going to come out," she said, holding up my bloody clothing.

"It is not important," I replied.

Just then the boys walked through the door.

"You must be starved from your journey," she said to them. "Supper is in the pot. You, too," she said to me. "But first scrub that blood from your hands and arms."

It took three washbasins of clean water to wash away the blood.

After my sons and I ate, Rachel tended my wounds by lamplight, gently washing the welts on my back and calf and applying a salve. I flinched from the sting when she touched the wounds.

"They are deep," she said. "They will leave lasting scars."

For the wound on my shoulder she made a poultice.

"Here, hold this against it," she said. "When will the healer come?"

I leaned close, pressing my lips to my wife's ear so that Avigail might not hear.

"No healer is coming," I whispered, and then looked into her eyes, shaking my head sadly.

"But I heard you say . . ."

"I tried," I interrupted, "I tried over and over, but none would accompany us."

She ran outside with her face in her hands.

I gave my wife some time to be alone with her grief before I went out into the moonlight to fetch her. We sat on a large stone with a blanket draped around us while I related what had happened to me. When I finished telling my story, she kissed me.

"I am glad you did not stay," she said, leaning her head against my good shoulder. "We need you here."

Then we went inside.

I kissed Avigail on her forehead before I blew out the lamp and then crawled into bed with my wife.

It was difficult for me to get comfortable enough to fall asleep. The stinging lashes made it unbearable to lie on my back. The wound on my right shoulder made it impossible to sleep on that side. My lower back ached, my calf hurt, and I was getting another one of my headaches. Eventually, though, I fell into a restless slumber accompanied by fitful visions and dreams.

I had flashing visions of being crucified, so disturbing in their horror and realness that I awoke in a sweat, frantically feeling for spikes in my hands and feet.

Rachel said, "It is only a dream, husband. Go back to sleep."

But *this* was one dream that I remember as clearly as I remember the day my mother died when I was a boy.

In the vision, I was sitting on a boulder in a brook with my feet in the cooling waters. From where I sat, I could see the shadows of trout waving above the pebble bottom. It reminded me of a place along the Jordan, but it was not. The sky was unlike anything I have ever seen. It was swirled with shades of blue, but it was also purple, red, and gold. The intensity of colors dazzled me. It was like looking into a pail of bright paints slowly stirred with a stick, only it was sky and clouds in the pail. And though it was day, yet there were stars in the sky. I recognized none of the constellations. Most fantastic of all, there were two suns in the sky, one noon high and the other rising over far mountains.

I was spellbound.

Along the creek, reeds and tall grasses and flowers swayed in a warming breeze. Their rustling sounded like music from chimes. Butterflies and bees and hummingbirds flitted from flower to flower, and flocks of small birds reeled across the iridescent sky. The green hillsides were speckled with white lambs and ewes. And behind me was a magnificent tree, its outspread limbs heavy with a strange, golden fruit I had never seen before, each as large as a fist. The lowest boughs reached down to the earth and then bent again toward the sun like wings.

The dappled shadow of the great tree was cast upon me.

As I sat, perfectly at peace and in awe of the sheer beauty of the spectacle, a light as blinding as the sun began to appear beside me. At first I was fearful and wanted to flee. But somehow I felt that the light would not harm me. In fact, I felt an abiding wellbeing I had felt only once before. I had a feeling that *love* resided within the light, that the light *was* love. I couldn't look directly at its brilliance. I held a shielding hand to my eyes and squinted.

Slowly, the light diminished to reveal the form of a man. I recognized him as the one I had accompanied to Golgotha, the man I had left to perish on the cross.

I lowered my hand.

But he wasn't the same man. Gone was the gouging crown of thorns, the bloodied garment, the battered face and eyes, the bleeding marks of the dreadful scourges and lashes. This man's flesh was unblemished, his clothes as clean and white as new-fallen snow.

He placed his hand on my shoulder and smiled.

"Peace be with you, Simon," he said.

I was startled. I did not recall having told him my name, and yet he knew it.

"Thank you for helping me to complete my obligation," he said.

"How do you mean?"

"I came to Jerusalem for the Passover, even though I knew it would mean my end. But my ending is also a beginning. It is the reason I came here. My struggle and my destiny was the cross, and you helped me along the way."

"You came to Jerusalem . . . to die?"

"As surely as the sun rises, and yet heartily I tell you I did not want to leave you," he said with the most sorrowful expression I have ever seen.

"Why are you sad?" I asked.

His eyes welled with tears.

"As I said, my death is only the beginning. I fear that multitudes will be killed *because* of my name, and worse, *in* my name, despite God's law not to kill, and contrary to the message I have carried as fervently as I carried the cross. I also fear that many will abuse my words and my message for their own gain, while others will use them to invoke hatred and oppression, masking their transgressions as piety. Human nature has an inexhaustible capacity to rationalize even the worst actions. Among the greatest of all human failings is shamelessness. Perhaps such a thing as Love is beyond human comprehension, as is the nature of God. Humanity will always be bound and limited by its nature, incapable of or unwilling to comprehend the larger purpose of its existence."

"But why did you come only to die?" I asked, not comprehending anything he had said.

"I came so that every person may have a close relationship with God, with *no one* and *no thing* to separate them.

"Are you speaking of the Temple and its priests and the barriers they construct for those who come to worship?"

"Do not judge them so harshly, Simon. After all, like us, they too are seeking to uphold the laws. Also, do not blame them. What happened to me *had* to happen. These are difficult times in Judaea. In their fear and uncertainty because of the Romans, the priests have become more concerned about avoiding conflict with Rome and protecting their own positions than sharing God's vision of love and forgiveness. They have lost their way. I did not come to abolish the laws. No, I came to take on the burden of the yoke and to bring an end to misinterpretations of the law and anything else that prevents people from experiencing God's love."

"Like what?" I asked with my brows furrowed.

"Like piety. Religious zealotry."

I was taken aback by his reply. How could being religious hinder nearness to God?

"But are not devotion and righteousness and Godliness things to aspire to?"

"Yes . . . And no," he said, pausing as if to collect his thoughts. "Oftentimes, the most pious are the most self-centered, including holy men and priests. They are in love with their piety, thinking themselves above everyone else until it is no longer God they love but themselves and their station above others. Their vainglory is their greatest sin. It is a disease that masks itself as humility. Be wary that your efforts to please God may really be blind ambition to set yourself above others or to condemn others, as if to say, 'Look at me! I am more pleasing than others in the eyes of God.' That person's prodigious zeal corrupts his or her ability to love others and fosters prejudice and dissension. Even your earnest prayers should be between you and God, like a secret, and not part of spectacle that you may be seen by other people. Your prayers should be humble and not exalted or full of empty words or phrases like the hypocrites who stand in the House of God and make themselves out to be the loudest and the most pious. God sees through their pretentiousness. You should pray *more* for others and *less* for yourself."

I thought of how much I had been praying for Avigail, begging God to help her. More than once, I had implored God to take me instead and to let my little girl live.

"You do not pray to *seek* God," the rabbi continued. "You pray to be *found* by God. Know that religious fanaticism is ruinous and poisons the well of love with disunity, setting one group against others, mothers and fathers against their children—all contrary to God's commandment to love one another."

I was dumbfounded. The things he was saying seemed contrary to what I had been taught.

"Are we not virtuous when we make God the center of our lives?"

"Yes," he replied, leaning close so that I could look into his eyes. "But conforming to what everyone else around you is doing is not the center of your life. The center is a personal relationship with God. Conformity annihilates that closeness, for you are always worrying about what others will think of you and whether or not you will be accepted. Faith is how we choose to live our lives, mindful that we dwell in the presence of God. It begins with the simple act of loving God. Because God loves you, you cannot have faith until you love yourself. It is a deeply personal thing. Hope cannot exist without faith. But know that true faith comes not from blind obedience to what others tell you, or even from what has been written, but from heartfelt reflection and questioning and a deep desire to experience for yourself God's immense Love. This questioning is sometimes called doubt."

"We should *doubt* the existence of God?" I asked skeptically.

"That is not what I said. Doubt is not disobedience to God. It is uncertainty that wells up from the wellspring of love and selflessness. Even the most holy men and women are sometimes full of doubt. There can be no path to faith without doubt. God does not want your blind obedience, for such a thing is as a shadow, without substance. It is a barren field."

The rabbi must have sensed my misgiving.

"I see you are suspicious," he said warmly.

I nodded.

"Then let me say this simply. Blind obedience is about closedness, not openness. Evil and tyranny prospers when doubt is stifled. Freedom exists only where doubt exists. That is why you were imbued with free will and curiosity, a desire, more necessity than thirst, to know the unknown, especially to know God. Indeed, part of faith is *un*knowing. If God but wanted blind obedience, you would not have been made with free will, doubt, and curiosity."

The things he said confused me. All my life I had been told to accept matters of religion without question.

Because the scriptures say so! the priests snapped whenever I sought answers or explanation.

"What you say confuses me," I said slowly, forming my thoughts. "I am not learned in such things. I am a farmer who cannot read or write. If I were an important man or a wealthy man, then perhaps I could . . ."

The rabbi did not let me finish.

"No!" he interrupted, though I would not say it was from anger or impatience.

Then he took a deep breath before speaking.

"Power and wealth do not bring one closer to God. That is why I have said that it is impossible for a rich person to enter the Kingdom of God, because that person sets himself or herself above the needs of others as if to say, 'Surely God loves me more than others because I have been given so much.' I say to you that the rich person has *taken* so much *from* others and gives nothing back. Rich people suffer from always worrying about their money. They worry about their expensive homes and possessions. They worry about robbers and kidnappers, about where they hide their money away, about how to avoid paying their fair share of taxes . . ."

I remember thinking that I did not worry about having too much money, but about not having enough money to support my family or to help my daughter.

". . . and about who will inherit their estate when they are dead and buried. The rich worry too much about their wealth instead of worrying about their neighbors. Whosoever shuts his heart against the needs of others does not love God. Good fortune does not imply God's favor; neither does bad fortune imply God's punishment. God does not want you to be rich. And power can turn a good man into a cruel and capricious man. Rich in wealth or rich in power, those who live for themselves alone do not live at all. They make an idol of prosperity. They build temples out of avarice. Worse, they are self-idolaters. Whosoever wants to be first in Heaven must be last and above all a servant to others. Mark what I say. God does not love the wealthy more than the poor or the downtrodden."

I remember thinking of the high priests in their extravagant robes rubbing their bejeweled fingers together in contemplation of the rewards of demanding twice the fee to sacrifice, and yet proclaiming that it is for God that they steal from and oppress their fellow Jews.

"But surely people can change." I said.

"All things are possible with God. True freedom to love God belongs to the one who is not chained and fettered by the world and by vainglory. Hence, the heart and mind is unshackled from everything other than God. That is why I have said, 'Blessed are the poor.' That is also why I said that I would not pray for the *World*. I meant the world in which people are assailed from every direction by the obsession to have more goods than their fellows, the world of buying and selling and profiting by any means, the petty and decayed world in which a person's value is measured by accumulated wealth. The world that pits us against one another, that exploits and enslaves some for the profit of others, and encourages the hoarding of resources by the few so that the many will not have enough. Such arrogance equates progress with profit and profit with righteousness, even though it destroys the world God created. People say they love God, yet they destroy everything they see as if they think God will make another world. It took God more than a thousand times a thousand thousand years to make this one. Was not one miracle sufficient?"

I remember thinking that when I first arrived in Judaea as a boy there were forests around Jerusalem. But now they have all been cut down to supply the timber needs of the ever-hungry city and the Romans who devour the world like locusts.

Just then the rabbi stopped speaking and nudged me with his elbow. He nodded for me to look at something downstream. A deer stepped nimbly into the brook to drink. It was unlike any deer I had ever seen. His pelt was reddish in the sunlight, his antlers enormous yet delicate. Suddenly, he raised his head as if startled, his eyes fixing on us, his ears swiveling forward, his tail twitching nervously. In an instant, he bolted from the stream to the far bank and vanished into the tall grass and reeds.

"Magnificent," we both said at the same time and laughed.

With the momentary distraction gone, the rabbi continued.

"When I said I would not pray for the world, I also meant the world in which politicians incite fear and hatred and divisiveness in order to convince others that they will save them if only *they* are given the power. They make false oaths and illusory promises even as they themselves craft the threats that cause the fear in the first place. These fearmongers believe if they tell lies often enough the masses will believe them as truth. They prey on ignorance and despair. But no matter how often or how fervently you say a thing does not make it true. They say they are on the side of God, but they blaspheme the name of God. It is only for themselves they serve, for they desire to be masters of the world. Do not be fooled. Those who exert power are never innocent. Power only protects the interests of those who wield it."

"Some things never change," I muttered.

"The world proclaims that it is God's wish for some to have more money and to have domination over others. In such a world money has become God. Doubtless, some arrogant kingdoms will even strike the name of God onto their coins as if to declare God's blessing for profiteering and money-making, extolling greed and selfishness as virtues. *I Want!* will be their creed. Know that all this is the opposite of God's will. This is my message to you. You cannot serve both God and money. All this scheming separates us from one another and does not unite us. It is driven by self-interest. Such things are as a dried up seafloor upon which nothing can grow for the salt. They do not fill up the empty heart. Even a gilded cup will not make you happy for long. It is the false promise of happiness . . ."

I thought of the people I knew who were never happy with what they had, who always said, 'If I only had *this* or *that* I would finally be happy.'"

"Do not be a slave to such stirrings. Desire to possess is blinding. Do not cling too much to anything in this world. Nothing made by people endures. Everything changes. Only God's love is eternal and immutable. Be wary of the pitfalls of piety. Do not wear your devoutness and virtue like a garment, for God sees that as pride. It is the *inward* expression of love that matters. You must look into your own heart. What you adorn your body with *outwardly* is of no consequence and does not prove love. Any person who does so holds no special favor with God. Anyone who does these things does so out of pretense and forgetfulness."

"What you say is true," I replied after a silence. "But is that not all the more reason that we *should* pray for the world, for its healing?"

I could tell the rabbi was contemplating my question.

"Perhaps," he finally replied. "Perhaps I have been hasty. Perhaps the world needs our prayers to redeem it."

"I have been thinking about everything you have said to me, about our weaknesses. Are we not less than God? Is not frailty our nature?"

"That is true," came his reply. "But humanity is strongest when armed with its frailty. The contents of your heart and your acts of kindness are all that matter. Compassion is the soul in action. Compassion triumphs because it is endless. A single act of kindness sends its ripple afar, all the way to God's infinite memory. Every stranger and beggar is sent from God as a test."

I thought of my neighbors, Jacob and Aliza, and of how often my sons and I helped them.

"I help others often, even when I cannot spare the time. My neighbor down the road owes me many favors," I remarked, a bit too haughtily perhaps, for his rebuke reminded me of the way my father used to look at me when I had said or done something wrong.

"Do not boast of the kindness you do unto others, Simon, for that is pride, but forget it immediately. Yet, never forget the kindness others do unto you."

I wished I could take back my words.

We sat for a while in contemplation, feeling the radiance of both suns and the gentle breeze that slid down from the lush, green hills.

I cannot say what he was thinking, but I was pondering the many things he had told me. I was struck by all his talk of how God loves everyone equally, for that was contrary to what other rabbis and priests had taught me. They were always talking about what *not* to do or what *not* to eat and who is reviled in the eyes of God.

Suddenly, I had a question.

"I have heard it said that God loves some more than others, that God even *abominates* some."

The teacher's reply was swift and stern.

"There is no one that God does not love. There is no one that God loves above others. Neither does God love one group above another, nor any nation above any other, for they are but constructs of humankind and are of no consequence to God whatsoever. What does God care of invisible lines drawn in the sand by violence and redrawn by violence in the blink of God's eye? You say you hate war, yet you dash into it wholeheartedly out of obedience or arrogance, be it individual, religious, or nationalistic. Is it so hard to turn your cheek? You lie if you say you love me and yet you would hate or harm others. All the vanity in the world is not worth a single life extinguished in hatred. Hate is an immense burden to bear. Do not presume to think you know what God abhors. God abhors those who oppress the rights and freedoms of others. It is written that God knew you in the womb. Therefore, God knew *who* and *what* you would become, and loves you still. *This* is what matters to God: Because God loves all equally, you must not turn your back on the needs or rights of others."

Listening to his words filled me with a sense of hope, but also of trepidation. I wondered if I had been living my life in a manner that pleased God. I wondered if Avigail's sickness was the result of my transgressions, as Jacob had suggested.

"I try to please God," I said. "I often deny myself pleasures that I may gain God's favor for my suffering."

"Do you think God revels in your self-imposed misery? Do you think you gain favor with the Everlasting One, the one Who Alone is Alone, because you deny yourself some simple joy, some sweet morsel? Did God not create those things for you?"

"But I have heard that some self-denial and austerity can be helpful," I said.

"That is true. Fasting can be especially useful for prayer and contemplation. It is also helpful to the body. But what loving parent demands that his or her children suffer merely for the sake of proving how much they love them?"

I thought of my children. I didn't wish any of them to suffer, least of all for me.

"It is not what you give up or deny yourself that matters to God. When I said to deny yourselves, I meant to deny your irrepressible pride so that you may love and serve others. God wants your mercy, not your sacrifice. How many times must I say this before you will hear me? Do your ears not hear?" he said, playfully tugging on my ear lobe.

"But how . . ." I said, stumbling over my thoughts, "how do I show God my love? How do I feel God's love for me?"

"You were created with a special place inside you that can always reach God. That place resides here," he said, touching my chest above my beating heart.

A hot tear ran down my sun-warmed cheek.

"Since we are made in the likeness of God, does God too have that same place?" I asked.

The teacher laughed.

He laughed a good deal. He seemed to embody joy.

"If I say that God is in everything and everything is in God, do you truly believe that the cosmic un-knowableness of God's mystery is confined in a single bounded form such as yours, with arms and legs and with ears that do not hear and with eyes that do not see? Where it is said that you are made *in* the image of God, I say that you are made *from* the image in God's mind, from the *imaging* of God's will, that is, from God's divine *imagination*. Creation springs from imagination. Because the image of God is Love, therefore, you are Love. That is how you are created in God's image. As God uttered a word and created the Universe, so

too a word was uttered to create you. The word was *Live* and *Love*.
You are the echo and answer of God's divine voice uttering the
Word. Through your eyes and hearts you are witness to God's
incomprehensible Glory."

I nodded slowly, as if I had begun to understand.

"You nod as if to say you comprehend, but no concept of
God held in the mind of man is sufficient to know God, no matter
how considered or reverent. It is arrogant to think you know what
God wants, either God's plan or God's will, for God is that which
is unknowable, infinite, and inexpressible. God's thoughts are not
your thoughts. Therefore, it is vanity to think you must defend the
honor and eternal Glory of God. No matter what name you give
God, God does not need to be safeguarded. God *Is*, regardless of
what humanity thinks or does. It is equally contradictory to say that
you love me and that you are a soldier on my behalf, for I am Love
not Hate. I am Peace not War. Do not impose your beliefs on others
by oppressing them or by making them to suffer. You cannot
compel others to love God, just as you cannot compel others to
love you. There is no love without freedom. God's message should
never be used to sow divisiveness. War and hate begins when
speaking and listening ends. The Eternal One does not reward
those who incite violence or kill in the name of God. Those who do
so act only out of selfishness and ignorance and

hatred, the roots of suffering and the source of separation from God. They would burn all the world on a pyre and say how they were doing God's work . . ."

I could tell from the way the rabbi was speaking faster and wringing his hands that the subject troubled him deeply.

" . . . I tell you now there is no paradise awaiting those who do so. There is no place for them in the Kingdom of Heaven. Love of God and violence are incompatible. The one countervails the other. I say it again: Do not kill, for all life is given by God. And do not glorify and make idols of those who kill. Whosoever kills, kills his brother. Those who insist that they know even the smallest measure of the impenetrable mystery of God deceive themselves and are self-righteous, and by their hands scatter the seeds of hatred and intolerance, the opposite of compassion and love."

"Surely that cannot be so," I said.

The rabbi lowered his head and shook it piteously before he continued.

"It is . . . and more. Such hatred is like a tenacious weed that even fire cannot defeat. I fear countless of my followers, as many as there are stars in the sky, will be incapable of seeing their own faults in what I am saying. Their hearts will dwell in the abyss of ignorance and hatred. They will be too self-absorbed with thinking that they alone are righteous and all else are wicked and godless.

They will be the first and the most vehement to complain about the faults in others, their fanaticism making them blind and deaf to mercy, mired in ignorance, and devoid of charity. They wrongly believe that right lies with whosoever shouts the loudest. They see the faults in others only because the faults they condemn are in themselves. Their over-attachment to blind convictions and stale rituals and lifeless words will make them oblivious to the kind of genuine love that brings us face to face with God."

Then he sighed and uttered something that has haunted me these many years.

"Sometimes I wonder if it was all worth it."

It troubled me greatly to hear him say such a thing. But I must admit that I too have often wondered what God finds in us.

"And though I gladly came for all this and more," he continued after a silence, "my mortal body was too weak from the scourging to continue. But you came along and helped me."

He put a hand on my shoulder.

I did not know what to say. I had not meant to help him at all. I just wanted to sell my wine and find a healer for Avigail. I would have gladly eschewed that duty.

"All that matters is that you *were* there when I needed you, Simon," he said, as if he had heard my thoughts. "*Your* strength gave *me* strength."

"Are you real?" I asked, touching him warily. "Am I dreaming?"

"Yes," he replied and smiled.

Then after a pause,

"And yes."

Seeing my confusion, he leaned close so that I could see in his eyes a kindness as radiant as the sun.

"Who are you?" I asked.

"I Am."

"But how can it be? The soldiers killed you."

The rabbi threw back his head and laughed. I loved it when he laughed. His laughter was so genuine, even childlike. It made me feel the way an infant must feel in the loving arms of its mother.

Then he smiled at me.

"They took nothing from me that I did not gladly give up, for God's hand was upon me from my birth. They did not slay me, nor crucify me, but it seemed so to them."

As I observed the man sitting beside me, his bare feet also in the brook, he shimmered like sunlight reflected on water, like a thousand sparkling diamonds. One moment he was perfect and without mark, yet in another instant, I saw the ragged holes in his hands, the crown of thorns, and the bloody lashes on his arms.

Sometimes he was both at once.

His form was like an ever-changing cloud sheared and shaped by the wind.

For a moment, we sat side by side on the boulder saying nothing, taking in the magnificent beauty of the place. My gaze fixed on the tree with the golden fruit.

"The tree is fantastic," I said. "I have never seen anything like it."

"I'm glad you like it. I made it especially for you, so that you would understand."

"Understand what?" I asked.

"The message I have carried. I am a door."

"How can one be a door? A door to what?"

"Have you heard the parable of the Wayward Calf?"

"No," I replied after thinking for a moment.

"Then let me tell it to you. There was an old man who prayed fervently that his soul would go to Heaven. Each morning during a great drought and famine he let his bone-thin calf graze in the withered hills, and every day the wayward calf wandered into a cave beyond a thicket of thorns; on the other side was Eden from which the calf ate of the lush grasses and drank from the sweet waters. And every day, when the calf returned late in the evening the old man whipped it, saying, 'It is wrong that I must go in search of you when I should be praying for my soul to go to Heaven.' At the end of the harsh summer the old man slaughtered the fatted calf and made a burnt offering of its tender heart. As he prayed on his knees at the altar, ash from the key to the Gate of Heaven fell on his shoulders."

"So . . . the old man should not have killed the calf?" I replied timidly.

"No," replied the teacher. "Instead of beating the calf, the old man should have *followed* it into the cave. Some people are so stubborn and so blind they cannot see when the door to Heaven is close at hand."

"So, you are saying that you are the door to . . . Heaven?" I replied, with a good deal of skepticism.

"Yes. I am also a light shining the way in the darkness."

"But you were crucified. I was there. I heard them hammering the spikes. How can you be a light or a door to anything?"

"Nonetheless, it is so."

Again, the man sitting beside me saw my failure to comprehend what he was telling me.

He took my hand in his.

"Love is a sheltering tree from the scorching sun," he said.

Then he pointed to the cool water flowing at our feet. He dragged his toes across the surface. A hungry trout, colored as a rainbow, came to the surface to investigate.

"Like water to the parched desert wanderer, God's love replenishes the thirsty soul. It is only by loving others that you shall be recognized as my disciples, not by memorizing and espousing scripture and obedience to laws to impress others with your piety—for that is *selfish* not *selfless*—but by the simple act of loving the world. Scripture that is recited without love is soon covered with dust."

I thought of all the people I had known who went about quoting scriptures as if to impress others, but who did not live by the words. All too often, they were the most unloving, uncaring, and uncharitable persons I had known, as if they believed hardening their hearts was to be virtuous.

"Love is not found in your stale and empty words, but in your actions. Faith demands actions of love. Be patient and kind with the young; show love and concern for the aged; offer sympathy and compassion for those who suffer and for those who despair, and afford solace to those who are helpless or in desperation, for at one time or another you will be all of these things. Love is the great, good use we make of one another. Without love you are as a flower without water. But remember, Simon, it is easy to show love and compassion to those who are close to you, to friends and family. The true measure of compassion is how much you love people who can do nothing for you, even unto those who do not believe as you believe—especially to those who do not believe as you believe."

Finally, I felt as though I understood something he said. When he said *love* and *compassion* he also meant to say *charity*. I would do anything for my family. I would give up my life for them.

"So love of others is the way to faith?" I asked, thinking about Avigail.

"Yes. But know, too, that the greatest faith is not by knowing how much you love others or even by knowing how much you love God, but by knowing that *you are loved by God*. It is by grace and mercy that God loves you, mercy within mercy within mercy. There is nothing you can do to merit such a love, and there is nothing you can do to have it withdrawn. Mercy and grace do not mean simply God's forgiveness of wrongdoing, they imply God's everlasting capacity for compassion. God loves you despite yourself and regardless of what you believe."

I felt powerful emotions welling up inside me, which can best be described as exultation and fear. The feelings were at odds with one another, for knowing that God loved me terrified me at the same time it filled me with jubilation.

I swallowed hard to hold back the rising feelings.

While the rabbi was marveling at the incredible sky bursting with shooting stars, he was laughing and clapping his hands in delight the way I have seen children do. I studied his face. In his ruggedness and thoughtfulness he was beautiful. His eyes were joyful and keen, as if nothing, however small, escaped their perception. Suddenly, I remembered what I had seen in his eyes when we were carrying the cross. This man, whoever he was, wherever he came from, was Love.

I smiled as I witnessed his delight when another shooting star raced across the sky.

"Did you see it?" he asked. "It is beautiful."

And it was beautiful.

Then he turned to me with a radiant grin.

"Love much," he said. "Laugh often."

Abruptly, the benevolent smile on the rabbi's face changed into a scowl of consternation.

"Anyone who abuses my message to obscure or impede truth, or who exploits my message to sow hate and intolerance, does not love me or God, though they swear they do," he said almost angrily, biting his tongue. "You think you look different and sound different from one another, but mankind is all the same to God, a Multitude of One. There is no *We*. There is no *They*. Such prejudice oppresses love and denies the inmost self. Where have I said to hate or to *exclude*? Did I not *include* women in my ministry, as well as adulterers, slaves, criminals, lepers and the lame, the demon possessed, the rich and the poor, the clean and unclean, and even those whose profession allows them to steal from the labor and sweat of others? Did I not show mercy to all who stood *with* me and *against* me? Did I not forgive my executioners and those who sent me to my execution? Have I not said to love even your enemy? Have I not commanded that it is wrong to judge others, lest you also be judged? Did I not caution against throwing the first stone of judgment, for once it is thrown the stone cannot be taken aback?"

"But do we not have laws?" I interrupted, thinking about a woman in a nearby village who was stoned to death last year for adultery. "Is it not our place to judge and to punish those who violate the laws?"

In answer he said, "How often are the innocent condemned out of treachery or prejudice or false witness."

It was not a question.

I remembered how the husband had at first praised the judges for upholding the law and his honor. But later it was revealed how he had boasted to a friend that he had lied about his wife to get rid of her so he could marry her younger sister. Even though the truth eventually came out, the faithful wife's life could not be restored. What use were praises sung to her bones? The thought that the scriptures had been used in such a vicious and calculated injustice made me angry. I wondered how many innocents had been killed in the name of upholding laws written by the fallible hand of mankind.

"No one is righteous in the eyes of God," continued the teacher. "Therefore, how can any person's judgment be righteous? Only God perceives everything. That is why it is written you must not kill, for each person is a unique and beloved creation by God. It is the sin that must perish, not the sinner. You save all humanity when you save or spare a single life. That is also why it is written that you must not bear false witness against others."

It dawned on me that those who judged the woman and those who eagerly cast the fatal stones were as guilty of murder as the conniving and lecherous husband, though I was certain they would each justify their wrongdoing in the belief they had done God's will and were therefore blameless.

In my mounting anger, I gritted my jaw and clenched my hands until my knuckles turned white.

The rabbi saw my apprehension.

He bent over and reached a cupped hand into the stream, and then he raised it for me to behold. As I watched, he splayed his fingers, letting the water spill away.

"Before setting off to judge others," he said, "know that your own sins issue from you like water pouring from an open hand. Do not be so eager to judge or to condemn others. No one is righteous in the eyes of God. Not a one. The book of my life must not be used as a sword or as a mallet with which to strike at others or enslave others or as an instrument of intimidation or prejudice, for I will judge those who do so. I will ask them when it is their time, 'Was that not you I saw who abused and mistreated another of my beloved children?'"

I remember that I was struck by his use of the word *I*. Surely he meant *God*.

Perhaps I had heard wrong.

"To be my follower is not a privilege," continued the rabbi. "It is a responsibility, a responsibility to love others, for God made love to be shared. The love you give to others is the only love you keep. It is only from loving others that you find your second self. Whatsoever you do to the least and most vulnerable of my brothers and sisters, you do to me. The Kingdom of Heaven will be built of love. That is why God created you with the desire to love and to be loved, a yearning felt deeply, especially in moments of stillness and in the quiet recesses of solitude where one can also discover the true self, unfettered by deception. Silence is like sunlight that illuminates the soul. But in the silence and emptiness can also be found the fullness of God."

For all his talk of love and compassion, I heard nothing that suggested this man could have incited insurgence or sedition as he had been sentenced. What violence or crime was there in his message? What was to be feared from this man? Was compassion unlawful? Was love treasonous? And yet this man suffered a brutal execution for it.

Suddenly, I thought about my daughter's suffering and about the woman who had been stoned to death and about whole peoples slaughtered off the face of the earth out of hatred, but also of the agony the teacher suffered at the hands of the soldiers who scourged and flayed him and hammered rusty spikes into his flesh. So much pain.

"Will you answer a question?" I said.

"If I can."

"You talk about God's infinite love and mercy. But if God is all-powerful and loves us so much, why is there so much suffering and evil in the world? Why doesn't God intervene and stop it?"

The rabbi looked up at the dazzling rainbow-colored sky, closed his eyes, took a deep breath, and then exhaled slowly. Then he opened his eyes.

"I wondered when you would ask that," he said without looking at me. "People *always* ask me that."

He hesitated before continuing, first taking another deep breath.

"My answer is two-fold. First, God created all things each with its own nature. A serpent cannot be anything other than a serpent. It is its nature. Neither can a scorpion or a spider be other than what they are. So too did God instill in Humanity its nature, which includes the kindled flame of good as well as the spark of evil. But out of love, God created you to enjoy complete freedom of choice."

"You mean it is up to us? We can choose to act out of goodness or out of evil and hatred?"

The rabbi nodded.

"It is never God's grace or mercy that is absent from the world," he said, "but humanity's . . . Always humanity's."

Then he tossed a small twig into the stream. We both watched as it drifted away.

"Secondly, and perhaps more important, Humanity's understanding of God is like a small boat adrift in the middle of a vast and tempestuous sea. You see only what is before you, the way the boat's prow cleaves the ceaseless waves as it blasts through each foaming crest, blown aimlessly by gales into the cloud-strewn horizon. But beneath the tumultuous sloshing sea, deeper than the highest mountain, lies a dark and unknown abyss, boundless and unfathomable, where leviathans lurk mindless of the storm above. The hapless craft is but a dust mote upon such thing. Such is your understanding of God. In your arrogance and near-sightedness, you think God's Nature and God's Will have been revealed to you and have ceased to be hidden. But God's infinite Being does not cease to hide, not ever, not under any condition, not for anybody. It is not in your nature to comprehend the fullness of God's Mystery."

I tried to imagine the tiny boat tossing on the wild sea. I wanted to understand. I was just about to ask another question when the teacher stood up from the boulder.

"My time has come," he said. "I must go now. But know that I go *because* of you, because you helped me to fulfill a promise. But I also go *for* you, because of God's infinite love."

I felt an overpowering desire to stay. The yearning was so consuming that I almost forgot my wife, my sons, and even my dying daughter. All I wanted was to be in his presence in this wonderful place.

"May I go with you?"

"None that live can go where I am bound," replied the teacher, with an expression that showed unease.

"Please do not leave me," I pleaded, grabbing the sleeve of his robe.

"I am with you always," he said. "I am as close to you as your heart. Every beat is the impulse of God's Will."

I took his hand and pressed it against my coarse cheek and then kissed it.

"Remember what I have told you," he said tenderly, his face beginning to glow. "Love one another. It is by love alone that we are judged. Our love. God's love. Laugh. Be joyous and allow others to find joy. Love kindness and humility. Love justice and seek it out. Help one another. Do not shackle your heart in the irons of indifference. Strive for peace in all things, for blessed are they who revere peace. Forgive others, for there can be no love or peace without forgiveness. No one is undeserving of forgiveness."

As he spoke, his entire body began to illuminate, as it was when he first appeared.

"Do not embolden ignorance and backwardness. It is no sin to reason. The pursuit of knowledge and Love of God are not contradictory, for God created you with a keen and curious mind. Know yourself and you will know God, for you are within God and God is within you. Love without fear, for love is the fulfillment of my message."

He was so radiant I could barely look upon him.

"Love God with all your heart. Life without God is empty and barren and rootless, laden with fear and futility and strife, and consumed with want and need for something of substance to fill the abyss of meaninglessness with a vital faith that is charged with the presence and love of God. The greatest sin is to refuse God's love."

Then he gently rested his shining hand on my head.

"Bless you, Simon," he said, his voice growing faint. "Your faith has healed you and your household."

I closed my eyes, feeling the weight of his touch, but also feeling lighter for it. When I opened my eyes again he was gone, and I was once again alone amid the splendor. Gone too was the tree. Instead, the cross that I had helped to carry stood in its place with the rising, golden sun crouched behind it, the long shadow falling over me.

Just then, the largest crow I had ever seen alighted atop the cross. With a steadfast glare of his black eyes, he cawed and cawed at me.

I took it as a sign.

Then I awoke.

For a long time, I lay in the darkness beside my sleeping wife feeling an unfathomable lonesomeness, as if I were separated from part of myself. More than anything in the world, I yearned to return to that sacred place in his presence. Finally, exhausted from my travails, I fell back into slumber.

I will tell you this about the vision: no matter how many years have passed, I have never been able to forget even the smallest part of it, as if the memory of it were engraved in stone. Never again did he visit my dreams, though I longed for it. Sometimes I wept from the longing. Often in my imagination, I returned to the refuge of the dream, though I do not fathom all of its meaning.

Perhaps you will do better.

Do not presume to find fault in what I have told you, for if it was but a dream, you cannot begrudge me what my mind does during sleep any more than I can begrudge you your dreams. If it was a vision, neither can you begrudge me that which was imposed upon me by another.

Saturday

"Love your neighbor as you love yourself.

There is no greater commandment."

Mark 12:31

I AWOKE IN THE MORNING TO THE FEELING of
something or someone crawling over me. When I opened my
weary eyes I could not believe what they beheld.

It was Avigail!

"Good morning, father!" she exclaimed, and she hugged me
around the neck and kissed me on the cheeks.

I nudged Rachel who was still asleep.

When my wife saw who was in our bed, she burst into tears
and scooped up our little daughter and held her to her chest,
kissing her head over and over.

"You are hugging me too tight!" Avigail cried, struggling to
free herself.

I joined in, kissing both their heads and weeping.

We took a good look at our daughter. No longer did she look
like she was at death's door. Her flesh looked healthy, her hair
lustrous, her eyes full of vitality, as it should be with a child of
four. Even the fever was gone.

"I'm hungry," said Avigail. She wriggled free of our embrace,
crawled over me again, jumped out of our bed, and ran to the
window to peer outside.

"It is a beautiful day. Can I play outside? Please!"

Rachel looked at me in disbelief and elation.

"It is a miracle!" she said. "How is this possible?"

Just then our sons awoke and saw their little sister standing before the window. They too couldn't believe it.

Avigail ran to their bed and jumped onto her brothers. They tickled her until she pleaded for them to stop.

"Let us go outside!" she begged, catching her breath and brushing her hair from her eyes. "It is so beautiful."

"After you eat something," said Rachel.

"Can we eat outside? Please, Mother. I want to feel the sun."

Rachel looked at me.

I nodded.

"Very well," she said, with a cheerfulness in her voice that I had not heard in a long time. "Let us get dressed first."

I sat up in bed, stretching my arms behind my head.

Rachel shrieked, startling me.

"What is it?" I asked, looking behind me, expecting to see a scorpion or a serpent.

"Your back! The welts are gone."

Rachel ran her hands across my back, not believing what her eyes saw.

"They are gone," she said again.

I reached around to feel where the lowest lash had been. I felt only smooth skin. I felt my calf. It too was healed.

My wife and I sat facing one another, dumbfounded.

"Avigail healed . . . My welts gone?" I said.

"How is this possible?" asked Rachel.

I shook my head.

"I do not know," I replied slowly, though my first thought was of the man I had abandoned at the cross, and who had visited me in my dreams.

Who was he? I wondered.

After our morning meal, I told Rachel that I was going back to Jerusalem. "I should return before nightfall."

"But why, Simon? Stay here with us, with Avigail."

"I must learn who the man was."

"Why?"

I told my wife of the astonishing vision I had during the night. Rachel was amazed by my description and by the completeness of my recollection.

"It sounds beautiful," she said when I finished. "But why must you go?"

"I feel *he* is somehow the cause of these miracles. I do not understand it myself," I said, shaking my head. "I cannot explain it. I only know that I must go."

Before leaving, I hugged Avigail goodbye and told my sons to continue to work on the goat house.

"Lay two more courses of stones. Use a plumb when you frame the window and door to keep the lines straight."

As was our tradition, my family watched as I walked down the road until I vanished over the hill.

My eagerness emboldened my steps.

I arrived in Jerusalem in good time.

The city was already bustling.

I began my inquiry with the guards posted at the governing house of Pilate. I thought the centurions who scourged and whipped the rabbi must know who he was.

I found three soldiers sitting and casting dice. They stopped and scowled at me. I recognized one of them as the scar-faced centurion from the day before.

"What do you want?" the man with the scar asked in crude Aramaic.

Most citizens of Jerusalem spoke some of the Roman's language, and they spoke some of ours, if only to command us.

"The man who was crucified yesterday," I said humbly, bowing my head slightly in deference, knowing that the centurions were quick tempered.

"What of him?" jeered one of the other centurions.

"Can you tell me his name and his crime?"

"What is it to you?" asked the scar-faced man, rising to his feet with one hand on the hilt of his sword. "Are you one of his followers?"

"No. I was the one who was made to carry his cross."

The centurion relaxed his menacing stance.

"I remember you now," he said. "I admired your strength."

I have to admit I felt a little proud that a centurion admired *my* strength.

"Go away," barked one of the other soldiers, taking up the dice.

"Please," I said. "What was his crime?"

"You're interrupting our game. Go away."

I persisted.

"Tell me and I will leave," I replied, a bit too haughtily for a Jew in the Roman Empire.

The third man, who had not spoken, looked at me sharply.

"They said he was King of the Jews, so I made him a nice crown."

The other two centurions sniggered.

I remembered the crown of thorns pressed into the rabbi's head, the deep gouges, and the blood-mopped hair. I wanted to jump on the man and pound his grinning face with my fists. But I held my anger. I hadn't come to Jerusalem to be arrested.

"His name," I said calmly. "Do you know his name?"

The scar-faced soldier shoved me brusquely.

"Enough!" he shouted. "Go away!"

I backed away for my safety, bowing and begging pardon for my intrusion. I would have to search elsewhere to learn the rabbi's name. But I had learned something from the soldiers.

Whatever he was, *whoever* he was, the rabbi was no criminal.

I stopped passersby on the streets, asking if they had seen the spectacle the day before. Some had. Some had not. Few of those who had witnessed the spectacle knew anything about the man, only that he was a criminal of some sort.

"I think he was an escaped slave," said some.

"I heard he was a traitor," said others.

"He is a thief who stole from the moneychangers in the Temple," replied one young woman who insisted her husband was present and witnessed the rabbi turn over the tables as he ran to escape.

A few said he was a blasphemer.

More than one said he must have been a murderer.

The stories were conflicting and incredible.

A man with four children said he had heard that the rabbi threatened to destroy the Temple.

Three people said they thought he was a Nazarene, but that was all they knew.

One said he was a prophet who had crossed Caiaphas, the high priest.

An old widow said he was a sorcerer.

But another old woman said he was a miracle worker who healed the sick and the lame, even lepers.

"He healed a man who had not walked in years."

Seeing my doubt, she declared, "I saw it with my own eyes."

I replied that healers were all magicians and swindlers cheating the sick and lame and weak-minded for money. They might as well be pickpockets. But the woman said the rabbi asked for no money, that he did so freely.

Her words struck me hard.

With all the different accounts of the man, I was sure I was not going to find the answer I was looking for.

But fortune was with me.

An old man pointed to a house down the lane and told me that some of the rabbi's disciples were staying there.

"I have seen them come and go," he said.

I thanked him profusely, pressing a coin into his palm before I set off quickly down the street.

I knocked on the door the old man had indicated.

No one came.

I knocked louder, almost pounding on it.

Finally, a man opened the door, only enough that I could see half of his face.

"What do you want?" he asked rather suspiciously.

"I'm looking for the brother of the man who was crucified yesterday."

The man opened the door wider and glanced up and down the narrow street.

"He's not here. You have the wrong house."

Then he tried to close the door, but I caught it before it closed.

"Please," I said through the crack. "I must talk to the one named James."

"What do you want of him?"

"I was with his brother yesterday."

The man opened the door enough to look me up and down.

"Wait here," is all he said before he closed the door.

I stood there for a time until he came back to let me in.

"Come. Follow me," he said, leading me up a flight of stairs to a large room.

Sitting at a long table was the man I had seen weeping and grieving on his knees the day before.

He recognized me as well.

"Are you the one named James, brother of the rabbi who was crucified yesterday?" I asked.

"Why do you want to know?"

"I have . . . questions," I said.

"I am he. Sit down," he said, motioning at a chair with a hand.

Then he turned to a boy sitting in the shadows who I had not noticed when I first entered the room.

"Bring us some wine."

"Excuse my manners," he said turning to the man who had opened the door and led me to the upstairs chamber. "This is Peter."

Peter nodded and so did I.

Just then the boy brought us cups and poured wine into them.

"And this is John Mark," said James. "He serves us and writes letters for us when we need them."

The boy looked to be about the age of my youngest son, Rufus. He was fourteen or fifteen, perhaps even sixteen, though he was much slighter in build.

"What do you want to know?" asked James, reaching for his cup.

"I was with your brother yesterday," I replied.

"I remember you. What is your name?"

"Simon. I am from Cyrene, though I have lived here in Judaea for many years."

"Why have you sought me out?"

"Please, I need to know your brother's name."

"His name is . . . *was* Jesus," replied James, correcting himself.

I whispered the name aloud.

"Jesus."

I felt a great unburdening in doing so.

"Tell me," said James. "How was it you carried my brother's cross?"

I told them how my sons and I had come into Jerusalem that morning to sell wine and to find a healer for Avigail. I related how I happened to be forced to carry the heavy cross and how the centurions whipped me as if I were a convicted criminal. When I related Jesus's desolation that his followers had all abandoned him, Peter wept.

I asked him the cause of his sorrow.

"I was a coward. I denied him three times, just as he said I would."

When I told him that Jesus forgave him, he wept even more, hiding his face in his hands.

"Love covers a multitude of sins, even my betrayal . . . and my shame," Peter said.

I told them how I left Jesus on Golgotha even as the centurions began to hammer the spikes into his hands and feet, because he urged me to leave for my own sake.

As I spoke, I noticed that the boy was especially attentive, fixed on my every word.

I told them how I passed two women and a young man on the way down the hill.

"Tell me, was one of the women an older woman?" asked James.

"Yes. She was with the young man."

James and Peter looked at one another and nodded.

"The old woman was our mother," said James.

I was horrified to think of a mother seeing her child die such a horrible death.

I went on with my story, telling them of my astonishing dream in which Jesus came to me in a paradise. I described the colorful, star-raddled sky with two suns and how the image of Jesus was ever changing, at once wounded, then perfect, and sometimes both.

They were extremely interested in this. They had many questions.

"Are you certain that is what he said?" they asked me each time I described another part of our conversation.

"Yes. I am certain. Every word."

I told them how in the morning Avigail was healed and the welts from my lashings were gone.

"I remember seeing a centurion whip you and your shirt bloodied," replied James. "Show me."

I raised my shirt.

Peter and the boy came closer to inspect me.

On seeing my unblemished skin, James smiled.

"The handiwork of my brother, no doubt," he said with tears in his eyes. "When we were boys, he healed me when a poisonous serpent bit me, and I was certain to die."

"How did he heal you?"

"He simply blew on the place where the serpent had bit me."

"How is that possible?" I asked.

"I do not know, but he always had such a power. He said it was from faith. With but a touch or a word I have seen him heal hundreds."

I remembered what the old woman on the street had said. I also recalled the last words of Jesus in the vision, that my faith had healed me and my family.

Did I have faith? I wondered. *Is that what I was feeling?*

"I too have witnessed many amazing things," added Peter.

"My brother told me often that faith alone is not enough," continued James. "He said faith must be accompanied by good works."

I recalled him saying as much in my vision.

"This Jesus did not seem to be a criminal," I said, after drinking wine from the cup and wiping my mouth with the back of my hand. "How did he come to be crucified? I have heard different accounts, none seeming true to me."

"Even before we arrived in Jerusalem," said James, "my brother prophesied that he would be tried and condemned and flogged and killed."

Peter began to tell of events of recent days.

"We arrived outside Jerusalem only a few days ago. The Teacher was talking to the multitudes. There were so many that he had to preach from the Mount of Olives outside the city walls."

"Afterward, we came into the city through the Golden Gate on the northeast side," interrupted James. "My brother was angry with the moneychangers and the traders in the Temple. He was outraged that the house of God was used for commerce and greed. He called the place a den of robbers as he turned over the tables and spilled their coin boxes."

On imagining the rabbi overturning the tables, my admiration for him grew. I had certainly wanted to do the same thing only the day before.

"He even threatened the destruction of the thing that stands between humanity and God," continued James. "I'm afraid he made enemies of the high priests, who could no longer ignore my brother's renown."

Then Peter said, "We ate supper in this room only two nights ago. Jesus sat in that chair," he said pointing to an empty chair. "He drank wine from the cup you are drinking from. He told us the wine was his life-blood."

I studied the tall clay cup in my hand, noting the imperfections from its firing. The vessel was as tall as the length of my hand, the base as wide as the mouth, and it was tapered in the middle for a hand grip. Exposure to uneven heat in the kiln had made it discolored—a dull yellowish brown on one side, a glazed richer brown on the other. The smooth inside of the chalice was of a greenish hue.

This had been his, I thought. *He drank his last drink from this cup.*

I held it tight, suddenly experiencing the intense yearning I had felt in the vision.

"During supper that night, Jesus told us that it would be our last," continued Peter. "He said he would soon die, and that one of us would betray him and all of us would abandon him out of fear. We strongly protested. 'Not one of us will do that,' we all proclaimed. Then Jesus turned to me and said that I would deny him three times. 'Not I,' I swore. 'I would never abandon you.' But I did . . . I failed him..."

Peter broke down.

James paused, respectfully. Then he began again.

"Later that night, we were resting in the garden on the other side of the Kidron beneath the light of a full moon when Temple guards came in the darkness."

"Peter told me to flee when we saw them coming," interrupted John Mark. "I managed to escape."

Peter said, "He is still a boy. I did not want him to be caught by the guards. I was afraid of what they might do to him."

James nodded in agreement before continuing.

"They arrested my brother and took him away to the Palace of Caiaphas where, we have been told, they convened a council of priests, though it was against the law to do so at that hour. They charged my brother with heresy and sedition. After sunrise, they took him to Pontius Pilate, demanding that he be executed. We were in the crowd," he said, glancing at Peter, "concealing our faces for fear that the mob would recognize us. Pilate sentenced my brother to be crucified when Caiaphas and his priests and the jeering crowd insisted. After that, you know more than we do."

There was one thing I did not know for certain, yet the vivid dream told me it was so.

"Did he die there?" I asked.

James and Peter looked down at the wooden table and nodded in silence.

"I thought so. I'm sorry I asked."

And I was.

No one spoke for a while after that.

Looking out the window, I noted that the day was getting late.

"I have to go," I said, standing up from my chair. "It is a long journey home."

Peter and James stood.

"Thank you for being with my brother at his end," said James. "You helped him."

"He said as much. May I keep this?" I asked, holding up the earthen cup that Jesus had used. "I can pay for it."

"Keep it," said James, "to remember my brother and what you shared with him."

I thanked him for the gift.

"I'm sorry about the loss of your brother," I said, as I clasped James's hand in friendship.

His eyes filled with tears. He nodded without speaking.

I also thanked Peter before I left.

As I walked down the stairs, clutching the cup, the boy named John Mark called down to me.

"Tell me again the names of your sons?"

"Alexander and Rufus," I replied without turning around.

"You said you come from Cyrene?"

"Yes," I replied as I opened the door to leave.

Once outside, I made my way through the crowded streets. Every face I passed, every face that looked at me without seeing, I wondered if that person had stood idly by and watched indifferently or with spite as Jesus struggled with his cross. I wondered if his death mattered to them, one way or the other. For my part, I would never be able to see Jerusalem the same as before.

I was tired when I found the road that would take me home. As I trudged along, thinking and questioning, my feet aching, I noticed that I hadn't had one of my debilitating headaches since the day before, since I had helped Jesus.

The headaches never came back.

I was exhausted when I finally reached home, having twice traveled back and forth to the city. The sun was low, perched on the cusp of the far hills. As always, I touched the mezuzah before passing through the door.

"Father!" yelled Avigail when she saw me.

She ran to me and hugged me around the waist.

"I missed you, Father," she said happily. "I am so glad you are home."

I bent down and kissed her head.

"And I missed you, Little One."

Rachel came over and hugged me and kissed me on the cheek.

"I am glad you are home, too" she said with a smile.

"Where are our sons?" I asked.

"They went to help Jacob dig a new well. I told them to return before sundown. They should be home soon for supper."

"They are good boys," I said.

I could smell supper cooking in the pot over the hearth.

"It smells delicious," I said. "I am famished."

Rachel kissed me.

"You must be exhausted. I will rub your tired feet before bed."

"Yes, I am very tired."

We ate as soon as my sons returned. Rachel instructed them to wash their hands first. I asked my sons about the work on the goat house.

"We laid *three* courses of stones, instead of the two you asked of us," boasted Alexander. "It will soon be ready for a door and the crossbeam to support the roof."

"All that and you still went to help Jacob?" I said, marveling at my sons' industry and good will and remembering what Jesus had said about helping others. "I am proud of you both."

But I knew that Alexander had another reason for going to Jacob's farm.

"And how was Nessa?" I asked.

Alexander blushed.

As we sat around the small table, eating a thick stew and sharing bread, I related to my family what I had learned from James and Peter.

"Did you learn the man's name?" asked Alexander.

"His name was Jesus."

My children repeated the name aloud.

Jesus.

I told them that he was a holy man and no criminal. I told them of his many miracles, including how he had healed the welts on my back.

I told my wife that my headaches were gone.

She smiled and squeezed my hand.

I said to Avigail, "It was *he* who healed you. You must never forget him."

"But how?" asked Rufus. "He never met Avigail."

"I believe it was when Avigail kissed my hand covered with *his* blood."

And then I showed them the cup. *His* cup. I told them what had been told to me, how he drank wine from it the very night he was arrested.

My family passed the cup around the table, each holding it with awe.

"Careful," I warned. "Do not drop it."

After supper, while my family readied for bed, I went out to see the goat house. In the darkness, I ran a hand across the stones. The boys had done a fine job.

Because I was so tired, I fell asleep quickly that night. But no sooner had I closed my eyes, it seemed, than I began to dream of the magnificent fruit tree turning into the cross. At first the cross was dripping with blood, *his* blood. I tried to catch it in the cup, *his* cup. But then blood poured from it like a torrent, threatening to drown me. I held my hands up against the flood and closed my eyes and mouth. I could not breathe. Suddenly, it stopped. I opened my eyes. The blood was gone. The cross glowed as if the sun shone upon it. No. It shone as if the sun was *inside* it, as if the cross was the sun.

Sometime around midnight, I awoke with the deep realization of what the cross was and what it was demanding of me.

It was God's mercy.

I got up and shook my sons.

"Wake up," I whispered. "Get dressed."

"Where are we going?" asked Alexander, rubbing sleep from his eyes.

Avigail stirred in her little bed, but did not wake.

"Back to Jerusalem," I said with a finger to my lips. "Go and hitch the donkey to the cart and fill it with straw."

To Rufus, I said to fetch a length of rope and two flagons of wine from the cellar.

While my sons dressed, I leaned over Rachel and kissed her on the head, as I often did to awaken her.

"Wha? . . . What is it?" she asked groggily without opening her eyes. "Is it morning?"

"No," I whispered, so as not to awaken Avigail. "The boys and I are going back to Jerusalem."

Rachel looked into my face through the darkness.

"Must you go at this hour?"

I spoke of the vision, telling her that there was something I felt compelled to do.

And though my wife begged me to wait until daylight, I told her what I had to do must be accomplished before sunrise. I couldn't explain why, but I felt its urgency.

Beneath a shadow-casting full moon, and draped in a warm spring breeze, my sons and I began the journey. As before, no one spoke as we trudged along half asleep; the only sound occasional yawns and the clip-clop of the donkey's hooves and the crunching of the wheels on the rough stone road.

Sunday

"Who abides in love abides in God."

1 *John* 4:16

WE ARRIVED IN JERUSALEM TWO HOURS before sunrise and went directly to the place where I had left Jesus. We secured the donkey and cart in bushes where they would not be seen in the dark. Two soldiers were sitting beside a small campfire when my sons and I came up over the hill.

Our approach must have startled them.

"Who is there?" one of them called into the darkness.

"Three weary travelers," I answered. "A father and two sons. May we come closer so that I may speak with you?"

"Come!" came the gruff reply.

Standing beyond the shadowy light of the fire, the soldiers looked us over. From where we stood, I could see the outlines of two crosses with corpses still on them. Undoubtedly, the soldiers were posted there to prevent the families of the two men from removing the bodies for burial. A cross lay on the ground near where Jesus had been crucified, but I couldn't tell if it was *the* cross. *His* cross. I would need a closer look.

"What do you want?" asked the taller of the two.

"Just a place to sit and rest and watch the sunrise," I lied.

"Go somewhere else," said the other soldier. "Jews aren't allowed here, unless you want to end up like them."

"Come, sons," I said, pretending to leave so that the centurions could see the two flagons of wine strung over my shoulders. "We will find another place to sit and drink our wine."

"Wait!" ordered the taller soldier. "Let me see those bags."

I handed him one of the flagons. He opened it, smelled it, and took a cautious drink. Satisfied, he smiled and handed the skin bag to his companion.

"I see no harm in sharing this place until the sun rises," he said. "Come and join us."

Before climbing the trail up to Golgotha, I had told my sons only to *make-believe* to drink of the wine. I told them that I needed them sober for what we were to accomplish. But I also warned them of the danger of what we were about to do.

"If something happens to me, you must get away and go home to take care of your mother and sister," I said sternly.

"But why, Father? Why must you do this?" my sons pleaded.

"Because my visions told me to," I replied. "I can't explain it to you."

As we sat down around the small campfire, I recognized the taller guard as the scar-faced centurion who had whipped Jesus and me, the one who shoved the young woman who ran out to wipe

Jesus's face, the one I had spoken to only the day before while he played dice with his comrades. Of the hundreds of centurions in Jerusalem, why did it have to be him?

My plan would fail if he recognized me.

But I was committed.

For the next hour, we five passed the flagon about, our reverie increasing as the flagon emptied. At one point I stood, pretending to stumble in my drunkenness.

"Where are you going?" asked the scar-faced centurion.

"So much wine. I must relieve my bladder," I replied, steadying myself.

The soldiers laughed as I made my way through the darkness to the cross lying on the ground. When the centurions were not looking, I got down close and searched for the knot and the tool mark. I was delighted to see that it was indeed the cross that I . . . *we* had carried. I placed a hand on it, feeling the familiar roughness.

When I returned to the merrymakers, I nodded to my sons.

After I sat down, the other soldier tossed a few sticks on the fire. As the fire blazed, the scar-faced centurion leaned toward me from across the stone ring, searching my face in the flickering light. I saw by his expression some dim recognition was forming.

"I have seen your face. Where do I know it?" he asked.

I said nothing, but leaned closer into the firelight, allowing him a better glimpse.

His eyes opened wide with astonishment.

My muscled tensed, ready to fight if I had to.

"You! The one who carried the cross."

I nodded.

"The same," I replied, my eyes narrowing as I slowly reached for the knife I had concealed in the leather straps of my sandal.

"What do you want with me?" he asked.

"Nothing."

"Why are you here then?"

I decided to tell the truth. My original plan was ruined.

"I have come for it," I said relaxing and nodding at the cross lying on the ground.

"The cross? What do you want of a hunk of wood?"

"I have had . . . visions," I said.

"What kind of visions?" he asked.

I could tell the centurion was sincerely interested in my dreams. I released my grip on the knife handle.

In the twilight, with dawn approaching, I recited the contents of my dreams to the soldiers. I told them of the paradise with the magnificent tree that transformed into the cross and of the miraculous healing of my daughter and the scars on my back. I told them that the man they crucified was no ordinary man and that the dreams urged me to safeguard the cross.

The soldiers listened intently.

"I too have had dreams," the scar-faced soldier stated when I was done. "The dreams began the night we crucified that man. They are so terrible I awake screaming. They are relentless. No sooner do I close my eyes than they return. I am afraid to sleep. Take the damned thing. I want no more part of it."

I seized the opportunity, rising and gesturing for my sons to follow me.

We separated the two beams of the cross. We could not risk being stopped. What would Roman soldiers or fellow Jews think of us hauling an instrument of so much horror? Alexander and I carried the upright beam, while Rufus carried the shorter cross member by himself.

I stopped beside the scar-faced soldier before heading down the stony trail.

"Thank you," I said, handing him the second flagon of wine.

He took it from me, acknowledging the gift with a slight tilt of his head and with a look in his eyes that could best be called . . . *regret*.

My sons and I started down the hill, but before we had gone a dozen steps I stopped and turned my eyes uphill.

"If it matters to you," I called out, "*he* forgives you for your part in his death."

Quickly, with no time to waste, we loaded the cross into the cart, secured it with rope, and covered as much of it as we could with straw. As we plodded along in silence, I wondered what to do with the two timbers once I got them home. I had not thought that far ahead. When we were a safe distance, I looked back toward Jerusalem.

The sun was already rising.

For thirty years after that, I visited James and Peter often in Jerusalem. We became steadfast friends. Jews and Romans alike came to know James as "James the Just," recognizing his virtue. I watched John Mark grow into the man known only as Mark. He was the first to write down the story of Jesus's life and death, the only one who had known him. He even mentioned me and my sons in his story.

Followers said the body of Jesus was gone when they went to the tomb on the morning I stole the cross. They said he arose from the dead and walked among the living. Some even avowed that he was the son of God. Others whispered that the high priest ordered his body to be removed so the place would not become a martyr's shrine. Others still said it was just James masquerading as his dead brother. But I knew them both, and I can tell you that James did not look enough like Jesus to perpetrate such a deception. I believe the stories that Jesus arose from the dead, because James and Peter told me how they saw him and spoke with him. I heard others did as well.

I am among them.

A few days after they found the empty tomb, I saw Avigail standing far off in the vineyard. She seemed to be speaking to someone, though from where I stood she looked to be alone. I called to her.

"What were you doing?" I asked when she came running up the hill to where I stood with my arms across my chest.

"I was talking to a man."

"What man?"

"The nice man in the vineyard," she replied happily. "He asked if I was feeling better, and I told him that I was. Then he smiled and said he was glad."

Her words concerned me.

"How many times have I told you not to talk to strangers?"

"Oh, but he wasn't a stranger. He said he was your friend. He said you helped him do something important and that he was the one who made me well."

When I went down into the vineyard to investigate, I saw no signs of him whatsoever, yet Avigail was certain she had seen and talked to a man.

That wasn't the only strange event in the weeks following Jesus's death.

Thirty days after I carried the heavy cross, I was hurrying home from Jacob's house one evening when I saw a crippled old man in rags sitting on the side of the road. As I passed, he held out an open hand seeking charity.

"Peace be with you," he said.

I walked by without hardly a glance or a word of kindness.

From behind, I heard him call out to me, "Do your eyes not see, Simon?"

I was startled. I had never seen the man in my life. I turned and addressed him sternly.

"What did you say?"

I saw that both of his eyes were clouded gray. I wondered how he could have seen me at all.

"Have mercy, friend," he replied. "Even beggars are sent by God."

"How do you know my name?"

"What you do to the least of your brothers," he said in a voice that sounded familiar, "you do to me."

I studied the beggar's face closely. I did not recognize him. But I was in a hurry to get home for supper.

"Here, old man," I said, reaching inside my tunic and removing a coin from my purse and pressing it into his open palm before I turned and walked away.

After a short distance, I remembered Jesus had said the same things to me. But when I turned to look, the old man was gone.

Take the encounter for what you will, but I know who I met on the road that day.

As for the rest of my story, my family became among the first followers of the teachings of Jesus. We attended many of their meetings at which they proclaimed the message of Jesus. Often was I asked to recite to those assembled how I carried the cross with Jesus to Golgotha and to describe my wondrous vision.

Those who listened were spellbound.

Many wept openly.

Over the years, I came to realize that the cross was a symbol not of suffering, but of selfless love.

I became one of their purveyors of wine and olive oil. My family prospered during those many years. When she was old enough, Avigail married one of the followers of The Way. But things changed after James was killed about eight or nine years ago. Those were dangerous times, full of whispers of rebellion. I heard that Peter was killed in Rome two years after that. I never knew what happened to Mark.

THAT IS THE END OF MY STORY. You may wonder how it came to be written. I realized that the new religion around Jesus was growing and spreading, and that I was part of the story, albeit a small part. I, who was with Jesus the day he died, who walked with him and suffered and bled with him, wanted to tell the news of what I witnessed that day—for that is what I was, a witness.

But I also wanted to tell you, warn you, that every smile and act of kindness and mercy you afford to others is Jesus's love shining through. Every judgmental scowl and effort to oppress the rights and freedoms of others and to cause suffering diminishes Jesus's love from the world. Jesus said there can be no love without freedom. Even the choice to love God must come freely. When Jesus said to love and forgive your neighbor and your enemy, he meant all people, everywhere, not just those who look like you or talk like you or believe as you do.

I know. He told me so. He was adamant.

Jesus's message was love, simply and invincibly love. He did not call upon you to be judges.

You deceive yourself if you believe otherwise.

We are each called to recreate Jesus's love in the world.

If God is in each of us, then it is through each other's eyes that we gaze upon God and God gazes upon us. Try to see what God sees in us.

The essence of Jesus's message was, more or less, the belief that each of us can be one with God, or at the very least we can diminish the distance between ourselves and God.

What did I gain from my experience, you may wonder?

I learned that possessing things cannot fill the emptiness inside you. Instead, strive to possess nothing, the entirety of it, and let love fill the void. By surrendering to the will of God, I found the deep shining peace Jesus spoke of, a peace that only comes from loving God. Jesus was a light, just as he had said. Light within light within light. I have often thought of the parable Jesus told me, the one of the calf and the cave and how some people refuse to walk through the door that leads to God.

But I have digressed too much from my story.

I apologize.

Last year the rebellion to expel the Romans failed. During the year-long siege, the Romans crucified ten thousand Jews in a ring around Jerusalem's inner wall. Eventually, the Romans took back the city and *Har Habayit,* the Holy Temple. They plundered the

Temple and hauled its wealth back to Rome. I overhead it would be spent to build a colossal arena. On the ninth of Av, they burned the Temple. The entire city was ablaze. I could see the glow of the fires even from my home. Afterward, the Romans dismantled the Temple and banished Jews and those who followed Jesus from Jerusalem, dispersed them into the wind like dust.

Fortunately, far enough away from the city, my family was allowed to stay on our farm so long as we provided a good portion of our wine and olive oil production for the large camp of soldiers, which was built outside the leveled city to ensure no Jews returned.

Times have been difficult since then, but my family survived.

Moreover, I am an old man who can barely walk or hear. My time cannot be far off.

Indeed, my sons have been taking care of their mother and me now that we are too old to take care of ourselves.

Concerned that the story of Jesus, and my small part in it, would be forgotten and lost forever, I asked my grandson to write it down for me. It no longer belongs to me. It is yours now. As I said at the beginning, perhaps you won't believe what I have told you. Perhaps no one will ever remember that a man named Simon from Cyrene helped a Nazarene named Jesus, a prophet and healer who some called the Messiah, carry his cross through the streets of Jerusalem and up to Golgotha where he was crucified and died.

THE YOUNGER SIMON'S SHADOW FELL across the earthen floor of the old goat house as he stood in the open doorway. His grandfather was sitting on a short stool prying the wax sealed lid from an ancient clay pot held between his legs. His cane leaned against the stone wall behind him. On the ground beside him were a large candle and a box of matches. From where he stood, Simon could see a hole in the ground that looked to be a little deeper than the pot was tall.

"Have you read it all?" the old man asked, without looking up from his work.

"I can't believe it. I have so many questions."

"Yes. It is true," replied the grandfather, anticipating the first.

"But, how? How did you come by it?"

The old man gently removed the lid from the reddish pot and carefully pulled out a papyrus scroll. He held it up.

"This is the original manuscript, written in Aramaic."

The young man came and knelt beside his grandfather, who carefully unrolled only a little of the yellowed and brittle manuscript, revealing the handwritten symbols in black ink.

"See? It's very old, almost two thousand years old."

"It's incredible," replied the grandson. "Where did you find it? Do you understand the importance of this discovery?"

"It is no discovery, Simon. It has been in our family for more than eighty generations, ever since the first Simon buried it here."

The young man was astounded.

"You mean . . . This is incredible! It's unbelievable! If this is real, it has to be one of the most important relics in history. Grandpa, this is huge."

The old man chuckled.

"That's what I said to my grandfather when he first showed it to me before your father was born."

"You mean you've had this for fifty years and you've never told anyone? This is important. It belongs in a museum."

"I know it's important," replied the old man. "That's why I'm showing it to you now."

The grandfather reached into the wide mouth of the clay pot and pulled out another object, wrapped in white cloth.

"For twenty centuries, our family has safeguarded this secret, no matter the shifting winds of politics. The first Simon, our namesake, who carried the cross with Jesus, began the tradition of passing down the story to his grandson so that it would be preserved. Ever since, a son in every other generation has been named Simon, and he becomes the guardian of the secret. When that Simon becomes very old, he passes on the responsibility to the next Simon, and so on. In such a manner, our family has protected the treasure for two millennia."

"What was the other manuscript I saw in the box?"

"A translation written in Greek a century or two after the first Simon died. After I received it from my grandfather, I took night classes to learn Greek at Hebrew University so that I could translate it. That is what you read. Although I was meticulous, I would say that my translation is very modern, especially in the way it refers to men and women equally, and the way it does not refer to God as a man or woman. I was as astonished as you must be when I first read it. This is our family's oldest tradition, Simon. As my grandfather passed it on to me, now I am passing it on to you. It is your birthright. You will inherit this land and the treasures it holds. You must not sell it or allow it to be sold out of the family."

"The whole thing is absolutely amazing," replied Simon, wondering what his grandfather meant by *treasures*. "It's incredible that our family has kept this secret for so long. Such a responsibility. Such faith."

As he spoke, his grandfather carefully unwound the long, white cloth from around the object in his hand.

"But maybe it's not ours to keep forever, Grandpa. Maybe it's time to share the story. The world could certainly benefit from it, now more than ever," continued Simon, thinking of the utter lack of kindness in the world, the greed and selfishness, and of all the oppression and violence inflicted in the name of religion.

"I thought you might say that," the old man replied with a smile and a wink as he finished unwinding the white cloth, revealing a tapered clay cup about as tall as the length of a grown man's hand. He turned it slowly, noting the differences in color and glazing, and the greenish hue on the inside.

The young Simon's eyes widened in recognition.

"Is *that* what I think it is?" he asked.

His grandfather smiled.

"Yes. It is the cup from which Jesus drank wine at his last supper when he proclaimed, 'This is my blood.'"

He handed the cup to his grandson, who cradled it in his hands. Tears formed in the corners of his eyes.

"This is the Holy Grail," replied the younger Simon, one tear running down his cheek. "I just can't believe it. It's so amazing. There really *was* a Jesus. There *was* a . . ."

The younger Simon stopped mid-sentence. He placed a hand over his mouth, stifling a gasp.

"The cross," he said breathlessly, as if the thought of it just dawned on him. "Whatever happened to the cross?"

The old man stood, placing a hand on his lower back and groaning as he rose to his full height. He looked up and placed a caressing hand on a long rough-hewn beam made of olive wood supporting the low roof, the upright of the cross that held Jesus. At the far end was a dark wedge of acacia wood fixed to the timber with a hole where an iron spike had been driven, the stained block upon which Jesus's feet were nailed.

Smiling, and with tears in his eyes, the old Simon stepped to the only window and touched the shorter timber across the top. It was the crossbeam onto which Jesus' hands were nailed.

Beyond the window, the setting sun shone over the darkening world.

Afterword

In a series of unlikely events, as I was finishing this book about historic Christian figures and relics—inspired in part by the writings of Thomas Merton—I discovered the simple, earthly possessions of Thomas Merton, including his white habit and black cowl and his iconic denim jacket shown on so many book covers. There were previously unknown photos, letters, and notes. It was one of the most important discoveries of Merton artifacts. Considered one of the most influential intellectuals, philosophers, Christian writers, mystics, and social rights and peace activists of the twentieth century, Merton's *The Seven Storey Mountain* is often compared to St. Augustine's *Confessions* as coming-to-faith autobiography. Objects from the collection are now housed at the Smithsonian's Museum of American History and the Thomas Merton Center in Louisville. The experience has given me unique insight into the awesome responsibility of safeguarding important religious artifacts and determining their ultimate disposition.

I did not take it as coincidence.

Interview with the Author

Canadian writer W. P. "Bill" Kinsella and John Smelcer were
friends since the mid-1990s. Kinsella's novel *Shoeless Joe* was
made into the blockbuster motion picture *Field of Dreams,* which
was nominated for three Academy Awards. His story "Lieberman
in Love" was the basis for a short film that won an Academy
Award for Short Films in 1996. Sadly, Bill passed away a week
after this book was published.

WPK: You say in the prologue that you were afraid of writing this
book. Why?

JS: There was always the persistent question in the back of my
mind: *Who am I to write this book?* This is one of the world's most
sacred topics. No matter how noble my intentions, I knew that
there would be people who would disagree with some aspect of my
vision. But despite all that, the vision persisted. *Simon. Jesus. The
Cross.* Write me!

WPK: And yet it took you twenty years to write it?

JS: There were always other books for me to write instead, many with the same theme of love and compassion and courage. And so it seemed easy enough to put aside Simon. It's pretty common for writers to abandon writing projects. But this story kept coming back. I will say that after working on the book for so long, I had a difficult time letting go of it. I kept tinkering with it even after I delivered the manuscript to the publisher.

WPK: What ultimately made you get serious and finish it?

JS: I worry about the future of humanity, about the world my daughters will inherit. There's too much hate and suffering, much it centered on religious intolerance, despite every religion's tenets of love, compassion, mercy, nonviolence, and charity. Too many people use religion to sow divisiveness and prejudice, to foster separation instead of unity, and to build walls between us, both physical and metaphorical. To paraphrase Robert Frost, be careful what you wall in or wall out. There are too many atrocities, large and small, inflicted against humanity every day in the name of religion. Jesus is called the Prince of Peace. When it came to violence his response was emphatic: *No violence.* Yet, it seems to me, his followers all too willingly abandon his directive and follow instead the drums of war. I felt the world needed to be reminded that Jesus's message was love and peace and mercy. I wanted to accomplish something beautiful and meaningful, something capable of challenging and affecting millions of hearts and minds. Because the desire for love, kindness, forgiveness, mercy, and peace is universal, *The Gospel of Simon* is a book for the world. That's why I sought help from people from other world religions.

WPK: I'm glad you finished it. It's a work of extraordinary power and resonance, especially with its timeless and necessary messages of love and compassion. I remember the day you called me in 2007 to tell me how you had died and how the doctors brought you back to life. I know you don't like to talk about the experience, but do you remember what you told me was your first thought when you came to in the hospital?

JS: Certainly. For years, I had been trying to ignore the insistent "vision" of this book, mostly out of fear and uncertainty. But when I awoke in the hospital bed, I remember an overwhelming urgency to write this book, as if my life depended on it. One close friend said I was given a second chance if only to write it. A priest told me he had a premonition that I was going to die that morning, so he stopped what he was doing and prayed that I would survive. I have been thankful every day since that terrible morning.

WPK: I'm glad you made it. I was worried about you. You once told me that the book had many different beginnings over the years. Can you give an example?

JS: For the longest time, the story began with the old Simon sitting on a stool in the goathouse with his extended family sitting on the dirt floor all around him as he recited the story of what had happened to him and Jesus almost forty years earlier. But I felt that version read like an artifact. I was afraid it wouldn't resonate with modern readers. I wanted readers to feel that Jesus was speaking directly to them and to our contemporary problems. The issue was resolved by setting the beginning of the story in present day Jerusalem. And without specifying the year, the story will remain fresh and relevant for years to come. It will always be *now*.

WPK: Jesus talks a good deal in this book, yet tradition seems to suggest that he spoke in short maxims like, "Blessed are the poor" and "Who lives by the sword, dies by the sword" and such. How do you reconcile the difference?

JS: Jesus was a preacher. He talked. Sometimes he talked a great deal, such as during the Sermon on the Mount, where Jesus spoke to an audience of five thousand for three days. He spoke for so long that the listeners ran out of food and became hungry so that Jesus had to perform the miracle of feeding 5,000 people with only five loaves of bread and two fish. The notion of Jesus uttering only terse sayings of wisdom is erroneous. What has survived in the gospels is likely a fraction of what he actually said—only those things that early followers remembered and found relevant to the growing religion around Jesus. Certainly he must have awoke some mornings, looked out the window and said, "Looks like it's going to rain today" or "Pass the beans" or "This is good soup" during a meal. Lastly, this is a novel. The fictional conversation between Simon and Jesus occurs during the ambiguous dream sequence. As such, a little poetic license should be permitted for the author to get his message across.

WPK: What would you say to readers who question if it's acceptable to write a book recasting a biblical story, especially one about Jesus?

JS: I would tell them it does not betray or subvert your faith to imagine what a conversation with Jesus might like or to contemplate his humanity.

WPK: You told me that there was a second part of your vision, aside from Simon's story. Can you say something about it?

JS: Not yet. I'm still wrestling with its profound implications.

WPK: Would you say you grew spiritually from the experience of writing this book?

JS: More than I ever could have imagined in the beginning. Although the general idea of the story came to me in a flash, my insecurities forced me to do a ton of research. It is no exaggeration to say I read more than one hundred fifty books on religion while writing *Simon*, as well as having countless conversations with religious clerics. I also enrolled in graduate courses in world religions at Harvard. In the process, I grew to respect and to appreciate the similarities and the differences between religions. Peace and understanding begins with listening.

WPK: You're clearly spiritual. Have you ever considered a life in the clergy?

JS: When I was a young man, I considered a vocation as an Army chaplain (likely influenced by M*A*S*H), but I felt like my true calling and true gift was to be a writer and teacher.

WPK: Were you surprised by anything while writing the book or while peddling it to publishers?

JS: My agent sent the synopsis of this book to the biggest Christian publishers in America. He included a dozen pages as a sample. No one even wanted to read the manuscript. Several publishers replied that no one would be interested in reading a book about Jesus's message of love and compassion and peace. I sure hope they were wrong. I was also astounded by the number of Christian friends who said they'd never read this book because it is praised by folks from other religions. Their closed-mindedness saddens me. How can there be religious tolerance and religious nonviolence if people are unwilling to listen to each other respectfully?

WPK: My last question is the most personal. What question does *The Gospel of Simon* answer in your heart of hearts?

JS: I *yearn* for a world where the messages that Jesus carried to us are ingrained in the fabric of our existence. Sometimes I weep for it. We pay lip service to them, but we don't live by them. If you don't believe me, just listen to the news and to the inflammatory speeches of politicians who, proclaiming their Christian-ness, incite hatred, divisiveness, oppression, prejudice, intolerance, and violence, despite Jesus's decree on the Mount that "blessed are they who are kind-hearted, who show mercy, compassion, sympathy, and who aspire to peace in all things" (Matthew 5:1-16). I think it's too easy to say, "I am saved simply because I believe in Jesus and God." I would think they want more from our faith than just our words. *Faith demands actions of love.* Jesus said as much. I long for a world full of joy and kindness and love and peace and healing and wholeness, a world where compassion and mercy is given to those who need it. *Our mercy. Our compassion.* To me, that is what Jesus meant when he said the Kingdom of Heaven was already at hand, right here, today, if only we would realize it. How bright the world would be if we were all ablaze by what St. John of the Cross called "the kindled flame of love." By writing *The Gospel of Simon*, I hope to share my vision of that glorious and sacred place, a world alight with the transforming power of mercy, where suffering is diminished, and where we love and care for one another to the fullest of human capacity. Your praise on the cover says this book is capable of changing the world. I hope you're right. But it can't do it alone. It needs the help of readers around the world who share the dream—one kindled heart at a time.

Help Spread the Good News of Simon

If you love this book—if it has affected you or deepened your faith—please help spread the word. Give it to friends and relatives, young and old alike, as a gift. Buy copies for your local library. Write a book review for your local newspaper or church newsletter, radio station, or favorite magazine. Write a review on amazon.com or goodreads.com or elsewhere online. Shout it out on Facebook. Tweet about it on Twitter. Post a short YouTube video. Send an Instagram of the book cover. Ask your local librarian to recommend it. Ask your local bookseller to order it. Discuss it in book clubs and Bible study groups. Recommend it on your church website. Invite the author to speak at your institution. Recommend it to your friends. Help make this book a word-of-mouth phenomenon. A portion of the author's royalties will be donated to charities. *The Gospel of Simon* is also available in Spanish. Learn more at www.thegospelofsimon.com

About the Author

John Smelcer, Ph.D., is the author of more than fifty books, many translated and published worldwide. His bestselling book of mythology, *The Raven and the Totem*, includes a foreword by Joseph Campbell (*The Power of Myth*). With Russian Orthodox Archbishop Benjamin, John contributed to the revised map of global Christianity in the 10th edition of *Living Religions* (Mary Pat Fisher, Ed.). With the Dalai Lama, John co-authored a poem on compassion. With astrophysicist and popular science writer, Carl Sagan (*Cosmos*), John had earnest discussions about science and religion. Dr. Smelcer's education includes postdoctoral studies at Cambridge, Oxford, and Harvard, where he studied Buddhism, Islam and Sufism, Jainism, Confucianism, Hinduism, Judaism, and Christianity, including the historical Jesus of Nazareth. He writes a blog encouraging religious tolerance and religious nonviolence for the Charter for Compassion. Learn more at www.johnsmelcer.com

Other Books by John Smelcer

Fiction

Alaskan: Stories from the Great Land

The Trap

The Great Death

Edge of Nowhere

Lone Wolves

Savage Mountain

Stealing Indians

Kiska

Native American Mythology

The Raven and the Totem

Trickster

Poetry

Beautiful Words: The Complete Ahtna Poems

Without Reservation

Indian Giver

Songs from an Outcast

Links

Like *The Gospel of Simon* on Facebook

www.facebook.com/thegospelofsimon/

or in Spanish

www.facebook.com/elevangeliodesimon/

Follow *The Gospel of Simon* on Twitter

https://twitter.com/gospel_simon

The official website *The Gospel of Simon*

www.thegospelofsimon.com

Official author website

www.johnsmelcer.com

CPSIA information can be obtained
at www.ICGtesting.com
Printed in the USA
LVOW11s1514020317
525947LV00001B/176/P